KT-116-962

The
Orkney
Book
of
Birds

Pocket Edition

by Tim Dean • Illustrated by Tracy Hall

First published in 2008 and now a revised pocket edition for 2011

Published by The Orcadian Limited (Kirkwall Press)
Hell's Half Acre, Hatston, Kirkwall, Orkney, KW15 1DW
Tel. 01856 879000 • Fax 01856 879001 • www.orcadian.co.uk

Text Tim Dean © 2008
Artwork Tracy Hall © 2008

ISBN 978-1-902957-46-3

All rights reserved. The contents of this book may not be reproduced in any
form without written permission from the publishers, except for short extracts
for quotation or review

Printed by The Orcadian Ltd, Hatston Print Centre,
Hell's Half Acre, Kirkwall, Orkney, Scotland, KW15 1DW

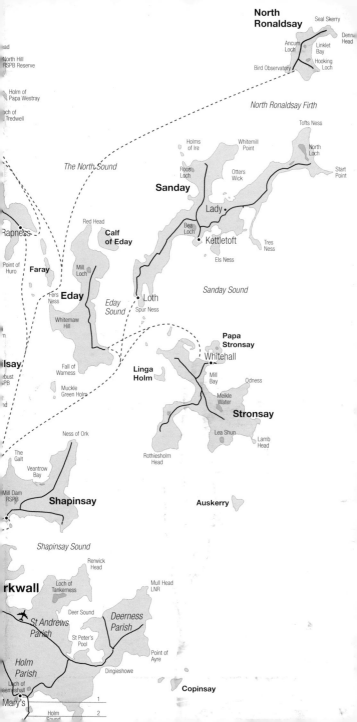

The Author and the Artist

Looking at birds has been a constant in **Tim Dean's** life for as long as he can remember. Since 1975 he has been paid to point them out to others - firstly in Wolverhampton as a teacher of children with learning difficulties, secondly in Cumbria with the Worker's Educational Association and lastly in Orkney with Community Education. In Cumbria he was the warden of South Walney Nature Reserve and Walney Bird Observatory for fourteen years. In Orkney he has worked for the RSPB, FWAG and SNH and feels that there are enough initials in the world. In both counties he has served time as the County Bird Recorder. This is his third book; the others are not bad either. Tim and Susan have a six year old daughter, Eleanor. She has a pair of binoculars.

Tracy Hall is an artist / illustrator and has been painting for as long as she can remember. She was born in Cornwall and eventually settled in Orkney in 1986. She paints flowers, wildlife and farm animals in no particular order but all in intricate detail. Her work is in private collections all over the world and has appeared in several books, magazines and ID guides. When she isn't working on a larger commission she prefers to look at the world through a magnifying glass; having discovered miniature art in the summer of 2007 she has already won several international awards for her tiny paintings including the prestigious Royal Miniature Society Gold Memorial Bowl in 2008. She lives behind an easel on the shores of Scapa Flow with her family.
www.watercolour-artist.co.uk.

Dedicated to our families, who probably now know far more about the birds of Orkney than they ever wanted to. Without their support and encouragement we would almost certainly still be on page one.

Acknowledgements

We are deeply grateful to the superb photographers who helped us out with additional reference pictures:

Brian Hewitt www.brianhewittimages.co.uk ;
Annette Cutts www.psiloswildlifephotography.co.uk ;
Sue Tranter www.suesbirdphotos.co.uk ;
Steve Round www.stevenround-birdphotography.com ;
Patrik Jonasson www.pbase.com/patrikjonasson ;
Glen Tepke www.pbase.com/gtepke ;
Mark Hamblin www.markhamblin.com ;
John Richardson www.pbase.com/rico101 ;
Guiliano Gerra / Silvio Sommazzi www.justbirds.org ;
George Reszeter www.birdphotography.co.uk ;
Richard Brooks www.richard-brooks.co.uk ;
Caroline Screech www.screechowlsanctuary.co.uk ;
Chris Edwards; Roy Thomson; Judy Schrader; David Andrews;
Robert Andrews; Tracey King.
Reference images for the Great Auk courtesy of the Natural History Museum, London.

Many other people have been incredibly generous with their time, assistance and local knowledge, and we would also like to thank:
Sally Banks, Chris Booth, John Dennison, John Fraser, Paul Hollinrake, Trevor Hunt, Michelle Koster, Alan Leitch, Eric Meek and Jackie Struthers. Thank you also to James Miller and Drew Kennedy at The Orcadian for their faith in this project and enthusiasm as it progressed.

Contents

Introduction

Why do it?

Most of my ideas are not the flick of a switch and eureka! variety. I now realise that it has taken a very long time for this book to come to life and I believe the route to have been something like this.

At the age of seven, my father bought me my first bird book, "Birds of Field and Forest" written by the exotically named O. Stepanek. Within its pages were paintings of colourful and extraordinary looking birds – Golden Orioles, Red-backed Shrikes, Woodchat Shrikes and Hoopoes. It fired me. At home in suburban Birmingham I was on a diet of House Sparrows and Blackbirds – I longed to see Stepanek's magical birds. There were fields and forests nearby – I searched them. My short-trousered explorations yielded Robins, Song Thrushes and Magpies and my imagination conjured up what must have been a Jay. Feverishly I filled in my I-Spy Book of Birds and was rewarded by five points for a Blue Tit and a guilty thirty points for that Jay. But why was I not seeing the Rollers, Wrynecks and Rock Thrushes so lavishly illustrated in Stepanek's increasingly well-thumbed volume? I continued the search for Alpine Accentors, Ortolan Buntings, Black Woodpeckers and Nightingales. One dark, warm June evening in a Midlands leafy lane I felt as though my hand had touched the Holy Grail; I heard the most wonderful and uplifting liquid song – it must have been a Nightingale. I now know it was a Nightingale but a few years later and out of short trousers, I realised in a resigned, grown-up sort of way that the fields were patches of urban Birmingham's wasteland and the forests were hawthorn hedgerows fringing canal sides. In reality there was little likelihood of seeing many of O. Stepanek's birds. His birds of field and forest bore little resemblance to Britain's birds of field and forest let alone Birmingham's. Further sobering reality revealed that the illustrations in the book were of stuffed, lifeless and glass-eyed birds, some of them unsympathetically engineered into bizarre and unlikely positions.

Twenty years later in 1979 and I am working for the Workers Educational Association in Cumbria; I'm grandly described as a tutor and my classes are called Birdwatching Walks in the Lake District. It is the start of a 30-year career sharing the joys and delights of bird watching. As I "tutored" my classes, I recognised that the O. Stepanek syndrome was alive and well. The "Workers", many of whom were new to birdwatching, devoured information.

The bird books of the day, the Collins "Guide to the Birds of Britain and Europe with North Africa and the Middle East" and the Hamlyn "Guide to the Birds of Europe" were stowed in their rucksacks and accompanied their birdwatching walks. Here we were in rural Cumbria and on a good day we might see 60 different species. Their bird books listed over 1,000 birds – they chorused their concern "how do we identify what we see when there are so many different species in these books? Where do we start? Beautiful though they are, we don't need pictures of Squacco Herons, Citrine Wagtails and Cretzschmar's Buntings. We want to be able to identify and learn about birds we are likely to see in Cumbria – Grey Herons, Grey Wagtails and Reed Buntings."

Wherever you are, Birmingham, Cumbria or Orkney, the same logic applies – the book needs to fit. Take for example my fictitious aunty in Evie who wants to identify the birds that come to her garden. It would be nigh on useless buying her a book entitled "Garden Birds" for it would be full of Blue Tits, Great Tits, Coal Tits, Magpies, Nuthatches, Jays and even Green Woodpeckers. In actuality, a roll call of my Aunt's garden in Evie would no doubt include Oystercatchers, Lapwings, Snipe, Linnets, Twites and even a dash or two of Hen Harrier.

What is it?

The number of different bird species that have been seen in Orkney is fast-approaching 400. Of these, almost 200 species have been seen less than fifty times and at least fifty of these species have been seen just once. Clearly it would be an indulgence to compile a book that illustrated the 400 – in so doing, the book would further perpetuate the O. Stepanek syndrome. My idea was to create a book of Orkney birds – a book that was specific to Orkney and which contained birds that were likely to be seen in the county during modern times, i.e. within the last 250 years. Consequently 200 or so species were immediately thrown out. Further rationalisation meant that the proposed book was reduced to 187 species – these species range from **very easy to find** birds such as Oystercatchers, Arctic Terns and Pied Wagtails to **very hard to find** birds such as Ospreys, Pomarine Skuas and Bluethroats. The first three are pretty familiar to everyone; the second trio are unfamiliar but occur in Orkney every year and can be seen if the appropriate knowledge, such as likely times and likely places, is utilised and sufficient effort is put in.

The illustrations

The next stage was to think about the illustrations – they needed to be unique. Local artist and friend Tracy Hall had both the skill and enthusiasm needed for such a major project. In a moment of madness she agreed to paint for the book. Inevitably the photographs, paintings or drawings in identification books are portraits of birds in isolation. *The Orkney Book of Birds* is different. Within this volume all the birds depicted are in a carefully chosen Orkney location and this setting has been selected either because the illustrated bird can be found there or because it has occurred there. This preparatory stage of the book was a very enjoyable exercise. Not only did it involve allocating the 187 species to Orkney backgrounds and ensuring an appropriate spread within the county, but it also involved visiting and re-visiting these localities in order to photograph the selected location for the bird. The essential element in this book was to ensure that virtually the whole of Orkney was represented. It would be perfectly easy to locate the birds in settings that covered just a handful of islands and parishes – a combination of Birsay, Hoy, Papa Westray and North Ronaldsay could have largely provided all the locations. However, all Orkney's parishes and all Orkney's inhabited islands are represented and a couple of formerly inhabited islands are thrown in for good measure.

Once the location had been chosen and photographed it was time for Tracy to create the paintings – or in her words, the unenviable task of translating my ideas into a reality. Although the germ of the book had been in existence for many years, it was only in March 2004 that Tracy and I started work on it. Initially we submitted three plates and three pages of text to *The Orcadian* in September of that year. We were given the green light – that meant just a further 47 plates for us to work on and a realistic target that would see the book published by Christmas 2008.

The text

Hopefully, and it's a big hope, each bird has been written about in a consistent and uniform manner.

The top line indicates the species name. I may be castigated for this but I've chosen not to use the names that are recommended by the British Ornithological Union Records Committee. Rather I've remained faithful to the older names that are still in common usage and with which most people are familiar. I would far prefer to read about Shelducks, Pochards, Eiders, Goldeneyes, Pheasants and Kestrels rather than Common Shelducks, Common Pochards, Common Eiders, Common Goldeneyes, Common Pheasants and Common Kestrels. Similarly, I prefer Dunnock to Hedge Accentor, Wren to Winter Wren and Robin to European Robin. Grudgingly I admit that there are a few new names that are better – Mew Gull for Common Gull and Black Scoter for Common Scoter are preferable (but I've still not used them!).

Where relevant after the species name I have included the Orkney or the Scots name. I considered this to be a fairly straightforward task initially. I scoured Gregor Lamb's "*The Orkney Norn*" and Charles Tait's "*The Orkney Guide Book*" and found a multitude of names for many bird species. Some of them are well known; *Bonxie* and *Tystie* are still in daily usage in Orkney. Others are less familiar and I've yet to meet anyone who is prepared to call a Hen Harrier a *Kattakally*. Some of these names are also more frequently used in Scotland rather than being confined to Orkney.

Following the species name there is a brief summary of **where** and **when** you might see the bird and the "**ease**" with which you might see it. The **where** simply contains a broad list of natural, semi-natural and artificial/man-made areas and habitats (see below) and the **when** relates to the four seasons. The **ease** with which the bird can be found is divided into six categories: **very easy, easy, not easy, hard, very hard** and **impossible** (remember that in these last 250 years the World and Orkney have lost the Great Auk). These categories sound fairly straightforward and in the main the system works well. There are always going to be anomalies though! Take for example Ring-billed Gull. As a species I have categorised it as **very hard to find** which in an Orkney context it undoubtedly is. However, anybody familiar with the Ring-billed Gull that has been a winter resident in Stromness since 1978 knows that if you go and stand by the lamp-post in Well Park near the Golf Club between November and February armed with a loaf of Mother's Pride or Argos' best then a Ring-billed Gull is (usually) easy to find.

Within each section there is information about the bird that places it in its Scottish or British context and also its Orkney context. Additionally in certain circumstances it's relevant to refer to its position in a European and world sense. The vast majority of the text concentrates on the Orkney aspect and includes appropriate reference to its history in the county, and contains more detailed knowledge of **where** and **when** you might see this particular bird and **how** you might be able to identify it.

The broad list of natural, semi-natural and artificial/man-made areas and habitats where a particular species can be found are as follows:

Marine

at sea
inshore
coasts
cliffs
shorelines
sand flats
mud flats
soft coast
maritime heath

Uplands

moorlands
upland stony slopes
upland gorges

Wetlands

lowland wetlands
lochs
lowland lochs
upland lochs
freshwater
saline pools
burns
loch edges
muddy freshwater
pools

Grasslands

rough grasslands
short grasslands
silage
hay fields
set-aside
cereal fields
cereal stubbles
ploughed fields

Woodlands

scrub
gardens

Miscellaneous

open country
towns
farms
farm yards
WW2 buildings
modern houses

The chosen localities

Auskerry   Storm Petrel

Birsay   Whooper Swan
                  White-fronted Goose
                  Shelduck
                  Mallard
                  Pintail
                  Pochard
                  Fulmar
                  Marsh Harrier
                  Hen Harrier • *summer*
                  Whimbrel

Burray   Common Scoter
                  Velvet Scoter
                  Little Tern
                  Great Grey Shrike
                  Twite
                  Brambling

Copinsay   Long-tailed Skua

Deerness   Ruff
                  Redstart
                  Barred Warbler
                  Whitethroat
                  Lesser Whitethroat
                  Yellow-browed Warbler
                  Lesser Redpoll
                  Common Redpoll

Eday   Cormorant
                  Arctic Skua
                  Stonechat
                  Garden Warbler
                  Spotted Flycatcher
                  Red-backed Shrike
                  Tree Sparrow

Egilsay   Spotted Crake
                  Lapwing
                  Arctic Tern
                  Skylark

Evie
Red-throated Diver
Sparrowhawk
Pheasant
Golden Plover • *summer*
Purple Sandpiper
Dunlin • *summer*
Snow Bunting

Firth
Goldeneye
Red-breasted Merganser
Goosander
Smew
Osprey
Woodcock
Swift
Goldfinch

Flotta
Rock Dove
Goldcrest

Gairsay
Red Grouse

Graemsay
Shag
Redshank
Curlew

Harray
Greylag Goose
Moorhen
Common Sandpiper
Sedge Warbler
Yellowhammer

Holm
Black-throated Diver
Little Grebe • *summer*
Red-necked Grebe
Grey Heron
Little Auk
Chiffchaff
Starling

Hoy
Barnacle Goose
Manx Shearwater
White-tailed Eagle
Buzzard
Golden Eagle
Great Skua
Dipper
Ring Ouzel
Crossbill

Kirkwall	Tufted Duck
	Black-headed Gull • *winter*
	Common Gull • *winter*
	Herring Gull • *winter*
	Great Black-backed Gull - *winter*
	Woodpigeon
	Great Spotted Woodpecker
	Waxwing
	Song Thrush
	Rook
Lamb Holm	Kestrel
North Ronaldsay	Sooty Shearwater
	Leach's Petrel
	Coot
	Turnstone
	Turtle Dove
	Lapland Bunting
Orphir	Pink-footed Goose
	Slavonian Grebe
	Peregrine
	Greenshank
	Grey Wagtail
	Dunnock
	Greenfinch
Papa Stronsay	Pomarine Skua
Papa Westray	Corncrake
	Jack Snipe
	Sandwich Tern
	Great Auk
Rendall	Merlin
	Common Gull • *summer*
	Meadow Pipit
	White Wagtail
	Whinchat
	Siskin
	Rosefinch
Rousay	Ringed Plover
	Kittiwake
	Razorbill
	Guillemot
	Raven
	Wren
	Willow Warbler

St Andrews
Brent Goose
Hen Harrier • *winter*
Bar-tailed Godwit
Short-eared Owl
Yellow Wagtail
Greenland Wheatear
Fieldfare

St Ola
Sanderling
Sand Martin
Carrion Crow
Hooded Crow

Sanday
Grey Plover
Red-necked Phalarope
Swallow
Rosy Starling
Hawfinch

Sandwick
Bewick's Swan
Water Rail
Golden Plover • *winter*
Green Sandpiper
Wheatear
Redwing
House Sparrow

Shapinsay
Ruddy Duck
Red-legged Partridge
Great Northern Diver
Common Tern
Blackbird

South Ronaldsay
Shoveler
Eider
Long-tailed Duck
Knot
Long-eared Owl
Cuckoo
Black Redstart
Blackcap
Pied Flycatcher

Stenness
Mute Swan
Black Swan
Wigeon
Gadwall
Teal

Stenness	Garganey
	Scaup
	Little Gull
	Mistle Thrush
	Chaffinch
Stromness	Little Grebe • *winter*
	Oystercatcher
	Dunlin • *winter*
	Ring-billed Gull
	Iceland Gull
	Glaucous Gull
	Robin
	Bullfinch
	Reed Bunting
Stronsay	Black-tailed Godwit
	Black Guillemot
	Bluethroat
	Icterine Warbler
	Linnet
	Corn Bunting
Swona	Rock Pipit
Westray	Gannet
	Herring Gull • *summer*
	Lesser Black-backed Gull - *summer*
	Great Black-backed Gull • *summer*
	Puffin
	Collared Dove
	House Martin
	Pied Wagtail
	Jackdaw
Wyre	Quail
	Snipe
	Black-headed Gull • *summer*

Birds in Orkney

Orkney is important for birds – fact. Many areas have been designated either because they are nationally or internationally important for birds. The nationally important sites are known as Sites of Special Scientific Interest (SSSIs) and the internationally important sites are known as Special Protection Areas (SPAs) and Ramsar sites. Quite simply SSSIs are some of the best places in Britain, SPAs are some of the best places in Europe and Ramsar sites are some of the best places in the world. Orkney boasts 38 such sites in total, 23 of them are the nationally important Sites of Special Scientific Interest and the remaining 15 include 13 Special Protection Areas and two Ramsar sites. A further indication of Orkney's significance is provided by the presence of the Royal Society for the Protection of Birds (RSPB) who manages 13 reserves totalling approximately 8,500 hectares of land. In addition Orkney has some 260 Sites of Local Nature Conservation Importance (SLNCI) with 185 of them recognized for their bird interest, and one Local Nature Reserve (LNR).

There are four major natural habitats in the county: sea cliff and shore, lochs and wetlands, maritime heath and upland (the hill) – the national and international designations include substantial tracts of these habitats. Orkney's eminence for seabirds such as Storm Petrels, Cormorants, Great Black-backed Gulls, Razorbills, Guillemots, Puffins, Kittiwakes and Arctic Terns is indicated by a lengthy list of sites that includes localities on the Mainland, both the North and South Isles and other remote and uninhabited off shore islands. Equally, the county's status for upland breeding birds such as Hen Harriers, Short-eared Owls, Red-throated Divers, Merlins, Great Skuas and Arctic Skuas is well illustrated by a similarly long list of designated sites and RSPB reserves which feature such bird species. These upland areas are confined to Hoy, the West Mainland, Rousay and Eday. The lochs, wetlands and shorelines of national and international importance support notable populations of breeding and wintering wildfowl and waders such as Pintails, Pochards, Tufted Ducks, Scaup, Goldeneyes, Ringed Plovers, Sanderlings, Bar-tailed Godwits, Purple Sandpipers and Turnstones. These wildfowl and wader sites include freshwater, grassland and shoreline from Sanday in the north to Switha in the south.

The full list of nationally and internationally important designated sites and RSPB reserves is impressive and serves to emphasise Orkney's significance for seabirds, upland birds and wetland birds.

Seabirds:

Auskerry SSSI/SPA – Arctic Terns, Storm Petrels

Calf of Eday SSSI/SPA – seabirds including Cormorants and Great Black-backed Gulls

Copinsay SSSI/SPA/RSPB – seabirds including Kittiwakes, Guillemots and Great Black backed Gulls

Holm of Papa Westray SSSI/SPA – Black Guillemots and Arctic Terns

Hoy SSSI/SPA/RSPB – seabirds

Marwick Head SSSI/SPA/RSPB – seabird assemblage, Kittiwakes and Guillemots

Mull Head, Deerness LNR – seabirds

North Hill SSSI/SPA/RSPB – Arctic Terns

Noup Cliffs RSPB – seabirds

Papa Westray SPA – Arctic Skuas and Arctic Terns (composed of Holm of Papa Westray and North Hill)

Pentland Firth Islands SSSI/SPA – Arctic Terns

Rousay SSSI/SPA – breeding seabirds, Arctic Terns

Sule Skerry SSSI/SPA – breeding seabird assemblage, Puffins, Shags, Storm Petrels and Leach's Petrels

Sule Skerry and Sule Stack SPA – seabird assemblage, Storm Petrels, Leach's Petrels, Puffins and Gannets

Sule Stack SSSI/SPA – Gannets

West Westray SSSI/SPA – breeding seabirds, Kittiwakes, Guillemots, Razorbills, Arctic Terns and Arctic Skuas

Upland birds:

Birsay Moors RSPB – upland birds

Cottascarth and Rendall RSPB – upland birds

Doomy and Whitemaw Hill SSSI – Arctic Skuas and Whimbrels

Hobbister RSPB – upland birds

Hoy RSPB – upland birds

Loch of Banks SSSI – roosting Hen Harriers

Glims Moss and Durkadale SSSI/SPA – Hen Harriers and Short-eared Owls

Hoy SSSI/SPA – upland birds including Red-throated Divers, Peregrines, Great Skuas and Arctic Skuas

Keelylang Hill and Swartaback Burn SSSI/SPA – moorland birds including Hen Harriers, Merlins and Short-eared Owls

Mill Loch SSSI – Red-throated Divers

Mull Head, Deerness (LNR) – upland birds

North Hill SSSI/SPA – Arctic Skuas

Orkney Mainland Moors SPA – Red-throated Divers, Hen Harriers and Short-eared Owls (composed of Glims Moss and Durkadale, Keelylang Hill and Swartaback

Burn, Orphir and Stenness Hills, West Mainland Moorlands).

Orphir and Stenness Hills SSSI/SPA – upland birds including Hen Harriers and Short-eared Owls

Rousay SSSI/SPA – upland birds, Arctic Skuas

Trumland, Rousay RSPB – upland birds

West Mainland Moorlands SSSI/SPA – upland birds, including Red-throated Divers, Hen Harriers and Short-eared Owls

Wetland and shorebirds:

Brodgar RSPB – breeding and wintering waders and wildfowl

East Sanday Coast SSSI/SPA/Ramsar – wintering waders including Ringed Plovers, Sanderlings, Purple Sandpipers, Turnstones and Bar-tailed Godwits

Lochs of Harray and Stenness SSSI/cRamsar – wintering wildfowl (Pochards, Tufted Ducks, Scaup and Goldeneyes)

Loch of Isbister and the Loons SSSI – Pintails and breeding bird assemblage

Mill Dam, Shapinsay RSPB – breeding and wintering waders and wildfowl

Onziebust, Egilsay RSPB – breeding and wintering waders and wildfowl

Stromness Loons RSPB – breeding and wintering waders and wildfowl

Switha SSSI/SPA – Barnacle Goose roost

The Loons and Loch of Banks RSPB – breeding and wintering waders and wildfowl

What the abbreviations mean……..

Site of Special Scientific Interest (SSSI) – National designation

Special Protection Area (SPA) – European designation

Ramsar – International designation (Convention on Wetlands of International Importance)

cRamsar – a candidate Ramsar site

Site of Local Nature Conservation Importance (SLNCI)

Local Nature Reserve (LNR)

Royal Society for the Protection of Birds (RSPB)

A 'stable door' thought:

Designating sites and creating nature reserves was prevalent during the last quarter of the 20th century. However, these twin protection measures were one year too late for Sanday's Red-necked Phalaropes, 25 years too late for Eday's Common Scoters, 89 years too late for Hoy's White-tailed Eagles and 160 years too late for Papa Westray's Great Auks – planet Earth mourned its loss soon after.

The Orkney Year

There is a predictability in the bird year that is constant and reassuring. We reaffirm our connection with nature and the year's cycle by our acknowledgement, expectation and recognition of these predictable events. Society in general has become less aware and less responsive to natural cycles and more sheltered from the subtle events that played a bigger part in the lives of previous generations. In Orkney, where so many activities and livelihoods are still totally dependent upon the movements of the earth, this remoteness from natural awareness is far less obvious. Many of the expected and reliable events, especially those of spring, are eagerly anticipated: the song of Skylarks (*Laverocks*), the displays of Lapwings (*Teeicks*) and Curlews (*Whaups*), the appearance of the Arctic Terns (*Pickies*), the rasp of the Corncrake. We delight in noticing the first nest building, the first eggs, the first chicks and flying young. All of the aforementioned are indicative of hope and a prosperous, fruitful season as the earth warms. It is always so much easier to notice an arrival; the departure is usually not recognized until the realization that something is no longer there. Equally predictable are the events that mark the earth's cooling: the sudden emptying of the cliff ledges, the arrival of large gatherings of Wigeon and Teal on the lochs, Long-tailed Ducks (*Calloos)* on inshore waters, swirling flocks of Snow Buntings (*Snowflakes*) on stubble fields and pastures filled with Curlews, Lapwings, Golden Plovers, Whooper Swans and Greylag Geese.

Of course there is also unpredictability in the bird year. Orkney's geographical location lends itself to unpredictable bird events. Migrating birds all too often encounter adverse weather conditions and if crossing water during inclement spells will make landfall at the earliest opportunity. During spring, southerly winds may occasion the arrival of overshooting birds from the Mediterranean while in autumn westerly gales may deposit visitors from North America and anticyclones over Scandinavia deposit waifs from Siberia. Winter, too, can witness unpredictable occurrences – severe northerly gales may bring vast numbers of Little Auks into Orkney waters, with less fortunate individuals being found moribund in gardens, under vehicles and sheds. It is not only the weather that produces these unpredictable phenomena; hungry European birds such as Crossbills and Waxwings use Orkney as a convenient stepping-stone between land masses, stopping to pillage and plunder before heading on.

Thousands of birds visit Orkney or reside here during the year. Despite the predictability of the bird year, it is impossible to give even an approximation of the numbers involved. We have calculated a few figures: we know that there are three quarters of a million breeding seabirds (Fulmars, Guillemots, Razorbills, Puffins, Kittiwakes and the like); there are 60,000 Greylag Geese and 1500 Barnacle Geese spending winter in the county; there are 130 breeding pairs of Red-throated Divers, 30 Hen Harrier nests etc. This is the tip of the iceberg – we have no idea of the number of Meadow Pipits that breed, no idea of the number of Twite that spend the winter and clueless as to the number of birds that use Orkney fleetingly during spring and autumn. What we do know though is that for most of these and especially for the regular breeding and wintering birds, Orkney provides food in abundance

Orkney is a county that has an established reputation nationally and internationally for fine food. Whether it's the raw ingredients from producers of quality or the imaginative creations from one of the many splendid restaurants and hotels, the list of accolades and awards is lengthening. Orkney beef, cheese, salmon, herring, oatcakes, ice cream, fudge, beer and whisky delight the human palate and though the recognition is well-deserved and increasing, it has only really developed in its present form over the last 20 years. On the other hand, for the thousands of birds that visit Orkney, they have known the importance of the islands as a destination for food since time immemorial. Consequently, depending on the season, there are birds in great numbers on sea, cliff, shore, loch, wetland, field and hill.

As the days lengthen, Orkney's wintering birds take the opportunity to fatten up before leaving for their summer breeding grounds. Huge numbers of Greylag Geese and much smaller numbers of Pink-footed Geese, Barnacle Geese and Whooper Swans compete with each other for the fresh new shoots of grass. The damp fields provide sustenance for waders such as Curlews, Lapwings, Golden Plovers, newly returned Oystercatchers and gulls such as the Common and Black-headed. Dabbling and diving ducks are numerous with Wigeon and Teal, Tufted Ducks and Goldeneyes on most lochs. Inshore waters still hold large numbers of visiting Long-tailed Ducks, Slavonian Grebes and divers plus large concentrations of more sedentary Shags and Eiders. Purple Sandpipers and Turnstones peck and pick without rest on rocky shorelines while the bills of Dunlin, Sanderlings and Bar-tailed Godwits probe the wet sand continuously. Set-aside fields and cattle feeding areas provide rich pickings for Snow Buntings, Twite and Rock Doves. As temperatures increase and the appropriate food appears, Meadow Pipits and Skylarks begin to reappear, as do Pied Wagtails and Lesser Black-backed Gulls. By the end of March Orkney's first summer migrants materialize in the form of Great Skuas, Sandwich Terns and Wheatears while April witnesses the arrival of the first warblers and Whimbrels, sees the return movement of thrushes to Scandinavia, the departure of the geese and Whooper Swans, and the build up of stunningly plumaged flocks of Golden Plovers.

The county's impressive seabird colonies begin to assemble during April reaching their peak in early June. Orkney's waters, where the warm currents of the North Atlantic Drift meet the cold waters of the North Sea, are a giant café. Vast concentrations of microscopic food attract fish, which in turn attract the seabirds. Food is abundant, as are nesting sites; the red sandstone cliff ledges provide the ideal safe location. If you have travelled via boat across the Pentland Firth, your appetite will have been whetted, either as you steamed through the maelstroms off Stroma and Swona where thousands of seabirds find a rich harvest or as you sailed past the towering cliffs of Hoy where thousands of seabirds nest. The Brough of Birsay, Mull Head Local Nature Reserve in Deerness and the RSPB reserves situated at Marwick Head in the West Mainland, Mull Head on Papa Westray and Noup Cliffs on Westray provide unforgettable views of Fulmars, Shags, Eiders, Guillemots, Razorbills, Puffins, Kittiwakes and Arctic Terns with the added bonus of marauding Arctic and Great Skuas.

The brown hills of the West and East Mainland, Hoy, Rousay and Eday are internationally important summer breeding grounds for moorland birds. Among the heather and surrounding rough grassland, the unique Orkney Vole can be abundant and plays no small part in the year's food cycle. Combined with a diet of rabbits and small birds such as Meadow Pipits, the vole population (although absent from Hoy) helps ensure the success of two moorland birds of prey, the Hen Harrier and the Short-eared Owl. From the birdwatching hide at Cottascarth in Rendall, you can observe Hen Harriers skydance in May and Short-eared Owls hunt to feed their chicks in June. The hills are also home to dashing and screaming Merlins, ground-nesting Kestrels and on Hoy, crag-nesting Peregrines. As daily dramas unfold for the main characters, all around can be heard the evocative bubbling song of the Curlew. On the tops, black lochans are home to Red-throated Divers and their spectacular breeding cycle rituals can be witnessed between April and August from the Burgar Hill hide in Evie or the Mill Loch hide on Eday – the latter site holds at least six pairs of "*loons*". The plaintive single-note calls of Golden Plovers and the trills of Dunlin are hard-earned rewards for visitors to the boggy summits.

At low level, the wetlands that teem with small fish, insects and succulent vegetation are brilliantly vivid with yellow flag, bog bean and meadowsweet. The available food and dense vegetation support upwards of 12 species of breeding duck, among which, with its British stronghold in Orkney, is the rare and elegant Pintail. Birdwatching hides at the Loons, Loch of Banks and Barnhouse in the West Mainland, Mill Dam on Shapinsay and Ancum Loch on North Ronaldsay afford the watcher unparalleled views of some of Britain's rarer breeding wildfowl including Pintails, Wigeon, Pochards, Shovelers and Gadwalls.

The cutting of silage commences during the last week in May and as summer progresses more and more Orkney fields are shorn of their grass and hay. These pale yellow fields of short grass become dining tables and attract birds immediately. The cutting provides easy access to abundant surface and below-surface food. The breeding season can be over quickly; for failed breeders it can be as early as that first silage cut. In subsequent weeks waders and gulls of all descriptions including adults, youngsters, residents and migrants, both successful breeders and failed, converge in their multitudes to peck and probe at this time of rural plenty. Many of these birds will remain in Orkney for the foreseeable future, for others this period of plenty is an opportunity to build up reserves before migration.

By August much has happened. The breeding season is well and truly over and many of Orkney's summer visitors have departed unnoticed. There is a sudden realization that species such as Arctic Terns and Lesser Black-backed Gulls are no longer here; they have melted away. The sea cliffs are empty except for lingering Fulmars and their well-fed offspring. The hills, too, have emptied – all that may be left are young Great Skuas still hoping to be supplied by their tired parents. In the wetlands, moulting ducks hide in the browning late summer vegetation; their plumage bearing little resemblance to that of their spring finery. Lowering water levels reveal muddy loch edges and freshwater waders such as Black-tailed Godwits, Ruffs, and, more rarely Little Stints and Curlew Sandpipers put in brief appearances. On overhead wires around farm steadings are impatient and restless gatherings of southbound Swallows.

It is about turn for many birds. September and October witness the massed return of birds from the north. The first Greylag Geese and Whooper Swans return in September and crop pasture which has just produced championship-winning cattle, and recently harvested barley fields. Likewise the Barnacle Geese fly in from Greenland on their annual pilgrimage to Switha and South Walls to spend the winter. The barley stubble and set-aside fields lure swelling flocks of Linnets and Twite and in turn this conveniently sized mobile food lures hunting raptors such as Merlin and Sparrowhawk. On exposed coasts, autumn tides have deposited banks of wrack and kelp that are alive with tiny seashore life. This attracts the rarely-still flocks of Dunlin, Ringed Plovers, Turnstones and Purple Sandpipers • many of whom will make the Orkney shores their winter home while others stop briefly for nourishment before winging further south. During this period easterly winds combined with rainfall often deposit large numbers of Continental birds – the county's east coast is the first landfall for migrants after their North Sea journey. Fieldfares, Redwings and Starlings can be found alongside each other frantically probing the soft Orkney soils for insects and grubs that will help them survive the forthcoming harshness of short winter days. The onset of these winds can signal frenetic activity among birdwatchers who, in pursuit of the rare, make their own migrations to the county's east coasts. North Ronaldsay Bird Observatory attracts binoculars from far and wide, the wearers of which are up with the lark and to bed with the owl, as they search for strays from the Mediterranean, Siberia and even America.

The lochs of Harray and Stenness become white with Mute Swans. The long summer days and warm temperatures have produced a feast of pondweeds to feed on. Companies of returning Wigeon, Mallards and Teal throng the lochs capitalising on the harvest. Upending Mute Swans have an attentive audience of Wigeon who sweep up any spilt crumbs. Tufted Ducks, Pochards, Goldeneyes and Scaup appear in their hundreds and Greylag Geese spend safe nights on the loch waters, after sating themselves on the still lush Orkney grass.

Even late in the year the seas provide food in plenty. Although most of the summer bird inhabitants have long-since departed to warmer waters, visitors from the Arctic have taken their places. Sheltered waters such as Scapa Flow, the Sounds around Eynhallow, Flotta, Papa Westray and Wyre become alive with the calls of the finely marked Long-tailed Ducks. These waters are also the winter quarters for species such as Great Northern Divers and Slavonian Grebes which have arrived from Scandinavia, Russia, Greenland and Canada while stressful oceanic weather occasions the appearance of seabirds including Little Auks, Gannets and Kittiwakes seeking food and shelter. It is often at this time in the year that food shortages on the Continent mean the coming of Siskins, Bramblings, Waxwings and Bullfinches to Orkney. They join the county's growing number of wintering Greenfinches and Chaffinches and find replenishment at the increasingly well-stocked garden feeders and sacrificial crop sites.

The Future

Despite this wealth of protected locations, there is instability in the bird world. Classification has secured most of Orkney's important breeding and wintering sites but securing essential food resources has proved more difficult to guarantee. In some cases the nesting areas now lie in splendid isolation, remote from food supplies and at the mercy of powerful forces such as global warming and the economics of agricultural development.

The impacts of climate change are difficult to forecast correctly. The breeding species most likely to be affected in Orkney are those that are close to the limits of their range. It may be that Red-throated Divers, Arctic Skuas and Whimbrels are lost as breeding species while Swallows continue to increase. The many thousands of wintering waders that use the Orkney coastline face an uncertain future with the prospect of rising sea levels impacting upon their feeding and roosting sites. Orkney's seabirds have been feeling the pinch over the last ten years and informed commentators have been pointing fingers at a number of issues, the most obvious being climate change. Over the last six years there have been successive seabird colony failures. At critical times in the breeding cycle it appears that sufficient and appropriate food is unavailable for Guillemots, Razorbills, Puffins, Kittiwakes and terns. Instead of gleaming succulent sand-eels with which to court partners and feed youngsters, the birds are forced to resort to less nutritious fare such as pipefish. Indeed Arctic Terns have been seen foraging for earthworms on damp roads. Recent years have seen tern colonies vacated by mid July; in many instances, young have been hatched but parents have been unable to supply enough good quality food for their survival. Seemingly for the same reason, Kittiwake colonies during the height of the breeding season yield half-built nests and aimless, loafing owners. What affects our cliff nesting birds also affects the Great Skuas and Arctic Skuas, both of which are experiencing hardship.

Agricultural changes have also played their part. The natural heritage of the islands has been shaped for centuries by low-intensity mixed agriculture. An eager emphasis on productivity encouraged by social changes and agricultural measures has eaten away this precious inheritance. "Improvements" such as reclamation of moorland and drainage of wetlands were the sparks that resulted in the designation and protection of the breeding sites. The county's wetlands, many of which are significant wintering sites for wildfowl, have been subjected to nutrient enrichment as a consequence of intensification and the increase in improved grassland. "Progress" has meant that farms have become more intensive and tidier while mixed cropping has declined. As a consequence many of Orkney's smaller birds such as Skylarks, finches and buntings have found food less abundant and less available. Yellowhammers and Corn Buntings have vanished from the Orkney landscape and we have witnessed the loss of almost all of the county's Corncrakes. A dwindling population of small birds touches the fortunes of Orkney's important populations of raptors such as Hen Harriers and Merlins, both of which have had recent and significant population downturns. It is to be hoped that adequately funded agricultural support schemes will help tackle this situation.

The Birds

Mute Swan • Lowland lochs all year; very easy to find

For much of the year pairs of Mute Swans tenant most lowland lochs in Orkney. The pairs are often long established and the male in particular patrols his watery kingdom possessively, constantly harrying any potential usurper that has the audacity to alight within vision on the water's surface. Fierce battles are characterised by the sound of slapped and crashing water and singing wings as the infiltrator is driven off. Substantial nests are built close to the water's edge and, by the end of May, often half a dozen cygnets are being chaperoned by their dutiful parents. The female, or pen, is slightly smaller than the male, or cob, and though both possess the black knob above the orange bill, the cob's is larger, especially in spring. Yet they have not always been common in Orkney. In the late nineteenth century, only the lochs of Skaill in the West Mainland and Wasbister on Rousay had their Mute Swans. During the 20th century however, following the introduction of pairs on some lochs for purely ornamental purposes, the species colonised rapidly and by 1983, the lochs of Harray and Stenness alone supported 36 nests. Nowadays there are in the region of 120 nesting pairs in the county and there are few islands without

Mute Swans (pen at her nest, cob offshore) and Black Swans in May at the southern end of Loch of Harray, Stenness • (l-r) Stenness kirk, Barnhouse hide and Ring of Brodgar.

a resident pair. Huge gatherings of non-breeding and wintering Mute Swans are a feature of the lochs Harray and Stenness and can involve as many as 500 birds. Nationally, the wetlands of Britain are important as at least half of Europe's population occur there.

Black Swan • Resident all year usually on either the Loch of Harray or the Loch of Stenness

One of Orkney's most well known birds is the lone Black Swan, which is frequently seen with Mute Swans on the lochs of Harray and Stenness. In the wild it nests colonially in Australia. However Orkney's bird is no doubt a refugee from a wildfowl collection and first appeared on South Ronaldsay in 1995 before moving to the Loch of Harray in 1997 via Echna Loch on Burray and the Loch of Ayre in Holm. In 2001, by way of North Ronaldsay and Shetland, a pair took up residence on the Peedie Sea before nesting and raising three cygnets at the Head of Work. In the following year they raised two young at the Mill Dam, Shapinsay but have not been seen since.

Bewick's Swan • Lowland lochs in autumn and winter; very hard to find

There are relatively few records of this species that closely resembles the Whooper Swan. It is quite possible that because of the similarity, its presence in Orkney may occasionally be overlooked. Both species have yellow and black bills but the amount of yellow on the Bewick's bill is reduced and more rounded. It is also smaller and stockier with a shorter and thicker neck. The lochs of the West Mainland seem to be the bird's preferential choice, but its occurrence is certainly not annual. Most of the sightings in Orkney have been of one or two birds, although five birds appeared on the Loch of Skaill in 1966. November and December are the likely months to see this species. The wetlands of Holland and East Anglia in England are the important wintering quarters for these travellers that have spent the summer in the wildernesses of arctic Russia.

Whooper Swan • Lochs, short grasslands and cereal stubbles in autumn, winter and spring; easy to find

This swan was once far commoner in Orkney than its cousin the Mute Swan. Records indicate that pairs of Whoopers frequently bred in Orkney before 1775 and that their chosen breeding sites were the very accessible holms in the lochs of Stenness and Harray. It appears that this accessibility was instrumental in the demise of the Whooper as an Orkney breeding bird. Eggs were easily obtained and sold southwards. Nowadays, the Whooper Swans that appear in Orkney during the winter have arrived here following a breeding summer in Iceland. During September herds, occasionally in hundreds and frequently including family parties, can be found on the lochs, pasture and stubble fields throughout Orkney. Some of these herds stay for the duration of winter and use traditional areas from one year to another. Others

Bewick's Swans (two adults) in November, resting at the western end of the Loch of Skaill, Sandwick – (l-r) Flotterston, Goldigarth and in the foreground West Aith.

4

only use Orkney as a fuelling stop before heading further south; seven months later they may re-use Orkney in April on the return flight to Iceland. They are widely travelled in the winter and may use several of Britain's traditional feeding sites, which include places such as the Ouse Washes in Cambridgeshire, Martin Mere in Lancashire and Caerlaverock in Galloway. A typical example involved a bird that was found dead in Stenness in the autumn of 1991; in the winter of 1989 it had been seen near Lough Neagh in Northern Ireland and at Caerlaverock while in the following winter it had turned up in Anglesey and County Down. In the summers in between of course, it had no doubt been nesting in Iceland. Surprisingly ringing has also revealed that birds from Finland sometimes spend winter in the county. One particular bird that was seen at Skaill Loch in Sandwick in 1999 had spent the previous winter in Cambridgeshire and East Lothian. Occasionally some Whooper Swans may spend the summer in Orkney; these are birds that may have been injured and are unable to return to their Icelandic haunts. Although as big as the Mute Swan, the Whooper has a much flatter head and a bill that is yellow and black rather than orange and black. Young birds, whose bills appear pink and black, show a dingier plumage. Whoopers spend far more time on land than the more aquatic Mute Swan and in general, any group of swans in a field is most likely to be composed of Whoopers.

Whooper Swans (three adults and three youngsters) during October, feeding in stubble near Twatt airfield, Birsay – background, HMS Tern and the hill of Yon Bell.

5

Pink-footed Geese in spring, feeding on the "first bite" at Gyre, Orphir – background, Gyre House.

Pink-footed Goose • Short grasslands and cereal stubbles in autumn, winter and spring; not easy to find

Like the Greylag, the status of the Pink-footed Goose in Orkney seems to have changed markedly in the latter years of the 20th century. Previously it was known as a regular passage migrant, skeins of which filled the September skies as they barked their way southwards from Iceland to the fields of northeast Scotland. It seemed they scarcely set foot in Orkney. In recent years they have become much more likely to be seen on the ground in the county. Although similar to Greylag Geese, increased familiarity will help in their identification – firstly, don't spend a lot of time looking for their pink feet. Their calls are more high-pitched and a lot less gruff than those of Greylags and their wings are a uniform grey – Greylag wings show a great deal of blue grey on the upper side. Pinkfeet become easier to identify on the ground. Those geese that look like they have a bright orange carrot attached to their heads are Greylags, while those geese that have a small chocolate head and a bill that has-to-be-looked-for are Pinkfooted Geese. In recent years, more and more Pinkfeet are being seen in Orkney either for the duration of winter or on spring passage. An indication of their wanderings is given by an individual that was ringed in northern Iceland in July 1998, seen at the Loch of Strathbeg, Aberdeenshire in

Greylag Geese during winter at Brough, Harray – background, Cuppin and St. Michael's kirk.

November of that year, resighted at Martin Mere in Lancashire in November 1999 followed by a March and April residency in Deerness in 2000.

Greylag Goose • Short grasslands,
cereal stubbles, lochs and at sea all year; very easy to find

It is hard to imagine an Orkney without Greylag Geese – nowadays they are such a constant part of the landscape both as wintering birds and breeding birds. However, it is only very recently that they have become the permanent feature that they are now. Groundwater (1974) stated that Greylags had not bred in the county and were not a common visitor to Orkney and, even as recently as the 1980s, there were barely more than 500 birds spending the winter. How different the picture is now. In recent years, numbers in winter have exceeded 50,000 birds; in 2007 they totalled well over 67,000 birds, substantially more than half the British wintering population. Many of these birds have arrived from Iceland lured by a generally frost-free Orkney that abounds with high quality grass to feed the high quality cattle. With such an abundance of food there is now no need for Greylags to expend extra energy in travelling further south. Indeed ringing has demonstrated many instances of birds that have moved to Orkney in mid-winter from their traditional eastern Scottish wintering grounds. Nesting birds can commonly be found on the hill, on rough grassland and on uninhabited holms and islands. They include the prolific descendants of goslings that were introduced to Shapinsay from Anglesey in the early 1980s and even birds from the native British breeding population from northwest Scotland have been found breeding in Orkney.

White-fronted Goose

You have to look hard at the finer points to sort out the different races and species of grey geese. Overall White-fronted Geese appear much darker than either Greylags or Pinkfeet; this is emphasised by the dark horizontal brown/black barring that extends across the lower chest and upper belly. The "white-front" refers to a small amount of white above the bill. There are two races of White-fronted Geese, the Greenland race which breeds in Greenland and the European race that breeds on the tundra of arctic Russia.

White-fronted Geese, eight Greenlands and one European (in right foreground), plus brown hare, during winter at Skorn, Birsay – (l-r) Quoylonga and the Loons RSPB reserve.

Greenland race • Short grasslands and cereal stubbles in autumn, winter and spring; hard to find

The vast majority of White-fronted Geese that come to Orkney are from Greenland and birds of this race have an orange-yellow bill. In the 19th century, this goose was considered to be "the commonest of the geese in Orkney, usually at the Harray loch". Nowadays there is just the one flock which rarely exceeds 75 birds. The most reliable place to see them is in Birsay where the fields around the Loons and Durkadale are the preferred haunts. Smaller numbers frequented the Loch of Tankerness, the southern part of Holm and Stronsay in the late 20th century. In Britain, the Greenland race chiefly occurs in Ireland and Scotland. Ringing has indicated that birds move between the main wintering grounds; this is clearly illustrated by an individual that was initially caught in Wexford, Eire then spent the following three winters in Islay and the next six winters in Strathclyde before being resighted in St Andrews in March 1997.

European race • Short grasslands and cereal stubbles in autumn, winter and spring; very hard to find

Each winter a handful of the European race appear in the Orkney fields. These birds have arrived from northern Russia and have a different coloured bill compared with their Greenland cousins. Instead of yellow it's pink but sometimes, in bright sunshine, the pink can look very yellow! It's a difficult bird to pin down and can be found in a whole host of localities. One sure-fire way of seeing a bird of this race is to look carefully at every goose in a flock. Eventually painstaking scrutiny will reap its rewards. Birds of the European race are chiefly found in England and south Wales.

Barnacle Geese during winter at Hackness, South Walls, Hoy – (l-r) Flotta, Martello Tower, Switha and Seaview.

Barnacle Goose • *Claik, Rotherock, Horra Goose* • Short grasslands and cereal stubbles in autumn, winter and spring; not easy to find

Birds from the Greenland population spend their winters in Ireland and Scotland and a visit to the southern end of Hoy between October and April should guarantee one of Orkney's most thrilling bird spectacles. The fields of South Walls are home in winter to a flock of over 1,000 dapper black, white and pearl Barnacle Geese. At dusk, they take to the air with yelping and high-pitched barks, and stream across Cantick Sound to spend the hours of darkness on the uninhabited island of Switha. It seems that these birds, in a flock that initially totalled 300, have been coming to the South Isles and using various islands in Scapa Flow since 1970. During the 1980s South Walls became the goose's preferred location and concerns relating to crop damage resulted in the setting up of the South Walls Goose Management Scheme. In return for providing feeding areas for the geese, farmers receive payment. Such has been the success of the scheme that it is still in existence and the flock of Barnacle Geese has increased slowly over the years and currently stands at 1600 birds. A few

Shelducks (drake standing, duck swimming) and five ducklings during late May in Birsay Bay, Birsay – background, the Earl's Palace.

Barnacles can be found throughout the county but no site is as regular as South Walls. Research has revealed that some of Hoy's Barnacle Geese are occasionally to be found on Islay, the wintering location of most of the Greenland population, while Islay birds are sometimes sighted on Hoy. Towards the end of September, skeins of Barnacle Geese are often witnessed flying south through Orkney skies. Some of these flights may involve birds from the Svalbard population – they spend winter on the Solway.

Shelduck • *Sly Goose, Ringer Goose* • Inshore, mud flats, lochs, short grasslands and ploughed fields in winter, spring and summer; easy to find

The large slabs of contrasting colour, black, chestnut and red, on its overall white body make the Shelduck one of the most easily identifiable of Orkney's birds and it can be found breeding in varying densities on most of the islands. They tend to nest in holes; consequently sandy areas with abundant marine invertebrates and accessible rabbit burrows are the most likely places to see Shelducks. During the winter and spring there are a number of sites in Orkney where loose gatherings of over twenty birds are common – these include Widewall Bay on South Ronaldsay, Mill Sand in St Andrews and the Ouse on Shapinsay. As the breeding season nears, pairs leave these areas for their summer territories that can include both coastal and inland locations. The black and white ducklings, like animated humbugs, are chaperoned constantly by their anxious parents during the first few weeks but are left to fend for themselves prior to fledging. The adults having had enough of parental duties fly to the Heligoland Bight to moult, to be joined by their offspring later. During late summer and autumn Orkney is Shelduck-less but by the beginning of November the sand and mud flats see the return of fresh-plumaged birds. For all but the moulting period Britain's estuaries, and increasingly inland freshwater, are home to Shelducks throughout the year.

Brent Goose • *Quink, Horie Goose* • Mud flats, short grasslands and cereal stubbles in autumn, winter and spring; hard to find

This is the smallest goose likely to be found in Orkney and has two races, the dark-bellied and light-bellied. Apparently Brent Geese have been visiting Orkney for many years but they are nowhere near as common as they once were. In the 18th century they were considered to be sufficiently numerous to merit commercial exploitation and were sold in Kirkwall for 4d or 6d. Brent Geese are very partial to a slender grass called *Zostera*

or eelgrass that grows in sandy or muddy sea shallows. Deer Sound, between Deerness and St Andrews, was one of the traditional Brent Goose sites and remains a place where they can still be found on occasion. Most sightings occur between October and May and the light-bellied and dark-bellied occur in almost equal proportions. Numbers are now small and sightings are widely scattered throughout the islands. Birds tend to feed in the intertidal areas when they first arrive in Orkney in the autumn but as winter advances, salt marsh, cereal fields and pasture are also used. It is not unusual to see them foraging on farmland, along with Greylags, in the thick of winter.

dark-bellied – breeds near the White Sea in northern Russia and spends the winter in eastern England

light-bellied – breeds in Svalbard, Greenland and Canada and spends the winter in Ireland and Northumberland

Brent Geese (two dark-bellied birds on the left, four light-bellied birds on the right) in October, feeding on eelgrass at Sandisands, St Andrews – (l-r) the Coastguard store, Taracliff and Dingieshowie.

13

Wigeon • Lochs in summer, lochs, inshore and short grasslands in autumn, winter and spring; very easy to find

In winter there are very few of Orkney's lowland lochs without a flock of Wigeon. The males are a splendid mixture of grey and white culminating in a chestnut head with a powder-yellow blaze; the females are a rusty grey-brown. In flight the white bellies are obvious and the broad splash of white in the drake's wing even more so. The males whistle; the chorus of whistling can be far carrying and on calm mornings and evenings is one of Orkney's most evocative winter sounds; the females growl. Groups of Wigeon start to arrive in September from their breeding grounds in Iceland, Scandinavia and Russia and by the end of October substantial flocks are a feature throughout the islands. Since they are dabbling ducks, they are mostly seen feeding in the shallows but can also be found in deeper water consorting with Mute Swans. They feed side by side; the swan upends and pulls up weed from the loch floor and the accompanying Wigeon feed on the vegetation that is disturbed in the process. Wigeon can also be seen grazing on short grassland next to open water. Some of Orkney's bigger lochs might hold as many as 2,000 birds and they are also numerous around Scapa Flow. There are probably no more than 500 pairs of Wigeon nesting in Britain, chiefly in central and northern Scotland; Orkney, with possibly 50 of these, is an important breeding locality and several lochs support one or two pairs.

Teal • *Ateal* • Lochs in summer, lochs and inshore in autumn, winter and spring; very easy to find

On many of Orkney's shallow lowland lochs where you can see Mallards and Wigeon, it's also likely that you'll come across the much smaller Teal. It's rare that you'll find this dabbling duck out in the deeper parts of a loch; they tend to hug the water's edge and feed in the shallowest parts among the shoreline vegetation. They are never far away from water and even when resting on dry land, they are invariably only one step away from the water line. Drake Teal are striking birds and in good sunlight are jewel-like especially around the head where the emerald green eye area is separated from the surrounding rich chestnut by a ribbon of yellow gold. Look out too for the cream yellow triangle at the drake's rear end. The females, like many of the dabbling ducks, are cryptically patterned with browns but in flight both sexes flash a broad bar of green. They are vocal birds and their soft musical and nasal notes can be heard during both day and night. As breeding birds they are widespread in northern and upland Britain; in Orkney, their nests can be found throughout most of the county in loch side vegetation, along the sides of burns and in wetland. As wetland in northern latitudes begins to freeze and food becomes less available, Orkney witnesses the arrival of many birds from northern Scotland, Iceland, Scandinavia and Russia.

Garganey • Lowland lochs in spring and summer; hard to find

This small duck has the distinction of being the only wildfowl species that is a summer visitor to Britain. A fraction bigger than its cousin the Teal, it tends to be found in the same types of habitat. Southerly and easterly winds in spring may bring a few of them to any of Orkney's rushy wetlands and favourite sites in the past have included the Loch of Banks, the Loons and Brodgar RSPB reserves and the Mill Dam RSPB reserve on Shapinsay. The female Garganey is very like a female Teal and is not easy to separate, but the male Garganey, with the dazzling white crescent above his eye, is a much easier proposition. It is possible that nesting takes place each year in Orkney, but they are secretive ducks so success is difficult to prove. As a breeding bird in Britain it is rare with no more than 100 pairs and, except for a small concentration in East Anglia, is scattered widely.

Gadwall • Lowland lochs all year; hard to find

This is one duck that you really have to try hard with; the Gadwall has the reputation of being easily overlooked. It's not the most obvious of our wildfowl; indeed, the female is easily confused with the very similar looking female Mallard. The male, though slightly more helpful, isn't that pre-possessing but close inspection reveals a subtlety of plumage that shouldn't be under-estimated. Overall he's a bird of different greyish tones with a very definite black rear end. This feature, plus the rectangle of white on the side, is the main pointer. On the Mallard-like female, the white rectangle is even more visible. In Orkney, the Gadwall is not an easy bird to find in summer or winter but is becoming easier. They first nested on Sanday in 1969 and since then have bred on North Ronaldsay, Shapinsay and several sites in the West Mainland including the Loons in Birsay, the Loch of Banks and Brodgar. In wintertime, pairs can be found lurking on a few chosen waters and flocks consisting of twenty or so birds are occasionally seen on the Harray, Stenness and Skaill lochs. In Britain the species stronghold is among the wetlands of southeast England.

Image overleaf . . .

Wigeon (duck and drake in left background on land), Garganey (drake in water in central background), Teal (drake in water in left foreground, duck in water behind,) Gadwall (drake in water in right foreground, duck in water behind), in

late May on wetlands near the Dyke of Sean on the Stenness and Sandwick parish boundary – (l-r) the Stenness hills of South Rusky, Mid Hill and Pullan with the Ring of Brodgar and Salt Knowe in the foreground.

Mallards (drake in the foreground, duck behind) during early spring near Walkerhouse on the Boardhouse Burn, Birsay – background, the Earl's Palace.

Mallard • *Stock Duck, Wild Duck* • Lochs, burns and inshore all year; very easy to find

This is a most adaptable duck; its adaptability in both nesting and feeding accounts for its success and widespread distribution in Britain. It does however have a preference for lowland farmland and river valleys and is virtually absent from the highest ground. In previous centuries it was an integral part of the nation's diet and great numbers were taken – in a six-month period in 1790, the markets of London received at least 200,000 birds. Its present day abundance is indicated by the fact that game interests may take as many as 750,000 per year. Like most ducks, the male and the female look totally different; the male sports a bottle-green head, bright yellow bill and a grey back while the female, like many other female ducks, is a mixture of browns and buffs. This combination of colours, while not being spectacular, serves the female well when she needs to remain inconspicuous as she incubates her eggs. Mallards can be found all year in low-lying areas throughout the county. They are considered mostly to be a

Pintails (drake in the foreground, duck behind) during spring on the Loch of Banks, Birsay – (l-r) Ravie Hill, the Twatt kirk and the drill hall.

freshwater duck and breeding usually takes place close to a burn or loch. Mallards can be very early nesters and it is not unknown for breeding activity to be seen in mid February. Orkney's resident birds are reinforced by arrivals from both Scandinavia and Iceland and many stretches of water, both fresh and saline and small and large, can hold loose flocks usually numbering in the low hundreds. There are recent winter records of 700 at the Mill Dam and 850 at Vasa Loch on Shapinsay, 630 on the Stenness loch and 1100 in Scapa Flow.

Pintail • Lowland lochs all year; hard to find

With its large global population, the Pintail can be described as the world's commonest duck. However, not only is the male Pintail, with its white and chocolate head pattern and its pointed tail, one of the most striking and elegant of the dabbling ducks but also it is one of Britain's rarest breeders. The first record was of a pair near Inverness in 1869 and even now there are probably no more than 40 pairs in the United Kingdom. It's also an Orkney speciality – the county's contribution to this total may be as many as a dozen pairs. Pintails are quite catholic in their choice of nest sites and have been found in a variety of wetland habitats and in a variety

19

of localities throughout the islands. In the 19th century, Sanday appears to have been a favoured island. However, it is now out of favour and the recognised strongholds that Pintails seem to prefer include the low-lying freshwater marshes at the Loons and Loch of Banks RSPB reserves in Birsay and the Mill Dam RSPB reserve on Shapinsay. During spring, almost any suitable site on any of the islands could hold nesting Pintails judging from the wide selection of locations in which Pintails have been observed. In winter, the Orkney breeding birds are supplemented by visitors from the north and small flocks, usually of no more than 20 birds, gather in a wide variety of shallow waters. Within Britain, major wintertime concentrations occur at estuaries; some of the largest gatherings can be found on the Dee and the Mersey.

Shoveler • Lowland lochs all year; not easy to find

The male Shoveler is a fairly easy bird to recognise. Its combination of bold blocks of colour – chestnut, white and bottle green – can make the drake almost as readily visible as a Shelduck. However, there is less white in the Shoveler and this bird, with its huge and slightly ridiculous bill, hugs the water more than the upright Shelduck. The female is a different proposition however. She can appear to be just like a female Mallard, a female Pintail or a female Gadwall. It's only when the binoculars or telescope reveal the spatulate bill that you are certain. In Britain Shovelers are scarce in upland areas and most numerous on shallow lowland waters in the south. It's not a common breeding bird in Orkney but seems to be getting more numerous and widespread. In the 19th century it was considered to be rare although several pairs bred on Sanday, while in the 20th century, the population increased in Orkney and in Britain as a whole. David Lack in 1941 wrote of a "rapid increase" while Eddie Balfour in 1972 suggested that it was more common on the North Isles than on the Mainland. Nowadays, as a breeding bird, Shovelers are likely to be found breeding on many largish lowland lochs. In the wintertime small-sized flocks can be found in similar localities, although gatherings of up to 50 birds have been known on some of the North Isles. Many of our winter visitors have reached the Orkney shores from their breeding grounds in Russia as typified by a bird that was ringed on North Ronaldsay in September 1997 and found dead in Perm, Russia, 3500 kilometres away two years later.

Shovelers (drake on the left, duck on the right) in June on the Loch of Lythes, South Ronaldsay – (l-r) Tomison's Academy, St Mary's new kirk, Akademi.

21

Pochard • Lowland lochs in autumn, winter and spring; easy to find

The needs of this diving duck mean that it can be seen in the winter months on most of the larger freshwater lochs throughout lowland Orkney. Pochards are mostly vegetarian and their generally shallow dives are in pursuit of seeds, roots and tubers from such plants as pondweeds and stoneworts. Orkney's lochs, with their ample supply of food and being generally ice-free, are welcome winter havens for these ducks that arrive in September from Scandinavia and Russia. Male Pochards look very dapper. Their three main colours, black, grey and chestnut, are well defined and have a crispness and simplicity that, in bright sun, is noticeably striking. The female is markedly less so, and her range of colours, a mixture of greys and browns, is considered "insipid" in at least one recently published bird book. The size of winter flocks has diminished in Orkney; Groundwater talks of thousands on Hoy and Sanday and even as recently as the 1980s, the Loch of Boardhouse and the Loch of Harray were supporting up to 4,000 birds. Nowadays it is unusual to find a loch that supports a thousand birds. As a breeding bird, it is very rare and usually restricted to no more than a couple of pairs, the Mill Dam RSPB reserve on Shapinsay and Ancum Loch on North Ronaldsay being favoured haunts. There are no more than 400 pairs in the United Kingdom most of which are in Scotland and eastern England.

Pochards (three drakes and two ducks; drake in the right foreground, duck in the left foreground) during winter on the Loch of Boardhouse, Birsay – (l-r) top of the Brough of Birsay light, Hunto and Breck.

Tufted Duck • Lochs all year; very easy to find

Of the three diving ducks on these four pages, the Tufted Duck is by far the most common and can be seen on most of Orkney's lowland lochs in both summer and winter. They are rarely seen on the sea. Like many species of wildfowl, Orkney's winter population is far greater than its summer population. Every year as northern latitudes start to cool down, Orkney becomes the winter quarters for Tufted Ducks from northern Europe and these birds join forces with those that have made the county their home in the summer. The bigger stretches of freshwater contain the largest numbers so that lochs like Harray and Stenness may have well over 300 birds during the winter. However, as with the Pochard, Tufted Ducks have been far more numerous in the past and the big flocks of fifty years ago seem to have disappeared. In the 1960s it was not unusual to find more than 2,000 birds on the Harray loch. Identification is fairly straightforward. The drake, with an eye of brilliant gold, is mostly black with a broad white flank patch and sports a black pigtail (vivid light transforms the black to purple). The female's colour is a variety of browns and she occasionally shows a flash of white above the bill. It was first reported as a British breeding bird as recently as 1849 and since then Tufted Ducks have increased quite markedly. In some locations they nest semi-colonially and on St Serf's island on Loch Leven there are in the region of 400 pairs; Orkney has mirrored this growth and during July and August, broods can be located on many of the lowland lochs.

Image overleaf . . .

23

Scaup • Lowland lochs and inshore in autumn, winter and spring; not easy to find

Their name probably comes from the Scots word "*Scalp*" which means bed of mussels. This is the rarest of Britain's breeding ducks and in the past they have chosen Orkney as a place to breed. Currently, no more than ten pairs breed in Britain but, between 1954 and 1979, pairs with their youngsters were seen almost annually on Papa Westray, North Ronaldsay and in the West Mainland. Most of Europe's Scaup breed close to water in Scandinavia and Russia and a high proportion of these birds spend the winter along the Danish, Dutch and German coasts. In Orkney, Scaup can be found on any of the lowland lochs. However, they can be found most easily and frequently at the Harray and Stenness lochs where, between October and April, up to 300 birds may be found. Their chief wintering sites in Britain

Tufted Ducks (two drakes and two ducks; drakes in the foreground, ducks behind) during winter on the Peedie Sea, Kirkwall – (l-r) Fire station, St Magnus cathedral and Hydro station.

include the Firth of Forth, Islay and the Solway where feeding birds congregate near mussel beds. In times past waste grain discharges from distilleries and sewage outflows were a magnet for Scaup gatherings. At a distance, Scaup can look very like Tufted Ducks; closer scrutiny reveals not just subtle differences but differences that make you wonder why you hadn't seen them before. The males of both species look black and white; look again and you'll see that the drake Scaup's back is pearl grey. The females of both species look brown; look again and you'll see that the duck Scaup has a big white blaze between the bill and the brown feathering of the head. Sometimes it's difficult to see this; the birds are night feeders and exasperatingly they appear to spend a great deal of time sleeping.

Scaup (two drakes and two ducks; drake in the foreground, duck behind), during winter on the Loch of Harray, Stenness and Harray boundary – (l-r) Plumcake Knowe, the Ring of Brodgar, and Orkney Trout Fishing Association launch site.

Long-tailed Ducks (drake and duck in summer plumage in the background, drake and duck in winter plumage in the foreground; the drakes have the long tails) and Eiders (adult drake in foreground and adult duck behind plus a young male in the background) during April on the east side of the 4th barrier between Burray and South Ronaldsay.

Long-tailed Duck • *Calloo* • Inshore, saline pools and on larger lochs in autumn, winter and spring; very easy to find

Strikingly smart in all their plumages, Long-tailed Ducks spend eight months of their year in Orkney. The vast majority spend summer near the Arctic Circle where females incubate up to nine eggs. However, they have been known to nest in Orkney, the last time being 1950. Their journey south begins after the breeding season and by October, Orkney waters, both salty and fresh, support loosely gathered flocks of "Calloos". Some of the largest groups, often numbering hundreds, occur in Scapa Flow with Hunda and Flotta prominent. Journeys on inter-island ferries, most notably the Shapinsay, Hoy and Rousay boats, can provide stunning close views of the "*old squaw*" as it is known in North America. As spring approaches, courtship displays become increasingly frenetic. Their haunting calloo calls ring out far and wide on calm days and nights, and both males and females shake off their crisp winter plumage and don an equally crisp summer coat. Just a stone's throw from St Magnus cathedral, the Peedie Sea supports a large and vocal flock in April and May prior to the birds' departure north. Most of Britain's Long-tailed Ducks spend the winter off the Scottish coast • Orkney, Shetland, the Outer Hebrides and the Moray Firth support large numbers.

Eider • *Dunter* • Inshore and at sea all year; very easy to find

These robust sea ducks are twice the weight of a Mallard and can be seen throughout the year in all their different pied and brown plumage. They are a familiar sight around most of Orkney's coastline and are usually found in the more sheltered stretches of water. Only very occasionally are they seen on freshwater; a small but very faithful group of birds can be found on the Harray loch in April and May each year. On calm winter and spring days, the coo-cooing sounds from the "*Dunter's*" courtship displays are far carrying. Some of the largest spring flocks are found in Scapa Flow with gatherings in hundreds around Hunda and Flotta. During May and June a walk along a stony shore may be rewarded by a female Eider sitting tightly on a nest containing up to eight eggs which are cosseted by down plucked from the mother's breast. Some nests are located within metres of the breaking tide, but other nests may be far inland amongst heather on the hill. Once in the water, groups of ducklings, their mothers and unmated females (aunts) form crèches. After the breeding, the drakes and ducks form separate moulting flocks. Scotland is home to most of Britain's Eiders; the largest colony is at the Sands of Forvie. In addition, there are a few colonies in Northern Ireland and just a couple of localities in northern England.

Velvet Scoter • Inshore and at sea in autumn, winter and spring; not easy to find

Like its close relative the Common Scoter, this species is easily overlooked but does have its favourite haunts and tends to associate with Eiders and Long-tailed Ducks. It is normally a little bit easier to find not only because of its faithfulness to certain sites but also because it is more numerous than its relative. Look out for it between October and May at Rerwick, Echnaloch Bay and Quanterness. The male Velvet Scoter is a smart-looking bird and gives the impression of being bigger and darker than immature male Eiders but at times the two species can look confusingly similar. Look out for the patch of white on the closed and open wing when the Velvet Scoter is at rest, stretching or flying. Closer scrutiny will also reveal the bright white mark below the eye, and the two white side-of-head blobs on the brown female. During the summer, Velvet Scoters leave Orkney waters and journey to breed in the world's far northern latitudes. As with the Common Scoter, the Moray Firth is Britain's premier site and in some years may hold up to 8,000 birds.

Velvet Scoters (drake in the left foreground and duck behind) and Common Scoters (drake in the right foreground and duck behind) during April in Echnaloch Bay, Burray – background, Echna Mill

Common Scoter • Inshore and at sea in autumn, winter and spring; hard to find

Easily overlooked, this dark sea duck is not the easiest species to find in Orkney. The drake is black and the female brown with pale cheeks and a brown cap. Despite its name, it is nowhere common but is worth looking for in winter and during spring and autumn migrations. Even though it may turn up anywhere, including on freshwater, Common Scoters appear to prefer certain sites; Rerwick, the Bay of Firth and Echnaloch Bay are frequently utilised often associating with Eiders, Long-tailed Ducks and Velvet Scoters. During the summer months, the female nests amongst blanket bog in the world's northern latitudes but it is possible that some of the birds seen in Orkney may be part of the small Scottish breeding population. Indeed Common Scoters bred in Orkney on numerous occasions during the 20th century with the Loch of Doomy on Eday being the duck's stronghold. This site, holding up to 11 pairs in the 1940s, had decreased to two pairs by 1958 and none since. They spend most of the year off shore and two of Britain's most important wintering sites are the Moray Firth and Camarthen Bay.

Red-breasted Merganser • *Sawbill, Harle, Herald, Hair duck*
• Lochs and inshore all year; very easy to find

Throughout the year Red-breasted Mergansers can be seen inshore and on many of the lowland lochs. Usually they can be found in pairs or small groups although, after the breeding season, when birds are moulting and flightless, gatherings of fifty or more can be found in localities such as Echnaloch Bay or Hunda Sound. Both sexes have "spiky hair"; the male's head is bottle green while the female's is chestnut. From a distance the male appears black and white, the white composed of a slab on the side and a white collar above the tan breast. Below her chestnut head, the female is grey to the waterline. Often both show the expanse of white belly as they roll in the water while preening. The nest is on the ground, often in the middle of thick undergrowth or even at the end of a rabbit burrow. In Britain, breeding birds are widespread in a variety of freshwater and tidal habitats especially in the north and west, and during winter, birds from Scandinavia and Iceland supplement our population.

Red-breasted Mergansers (drake in the foreground and duck behind) and Goldeneyes (drake in the foreground and two ducks either side) during spring in the Bay of Firth at Finstown, Firth – (l-r) Finstown brig, Firth School and Scarva Taing.

Goldeneye • *Gowdy Duck, Kwink* • Lochs and inshore in autumn, winter and spring; easy to find

The Goldeneyes that visit Orkney have arrived from the lakes and rivers of the forests in Scandinavia and Russia. Usually they nest in deep holes in trees and on hatching the ducklings tumble to the ground from considerable heights and make a perilous overland journey to water. They are not as numerous as some of the wintering wildfowl but are widespread and from October can be found, usually in loose flocks, on most lochs and inshore waters. The largest lochs hold the highest numbers; the Stenness loch sometimes has as many as 300. The male and female, with their triangular-shaped heads, sport very different but smart plumages; the drake is black and white with liberal white spotting, including a white tear on his cheek, while the grey duck's chocolate-brown head sits on top of a clerical white collar. As summer approaches, the males engage in extravagant posturing and head-throwing displays. Goldeneyes were first discovered breeding in Britain in 1970, since then the population has increased rapidly and now about 200 pairs breed, mainly in nest boxes, in the Strathspey region.

Smew • Lochs in autumn, winter and spring; very hard to find

This is the smallest sawbill. The male, with his neat and crisp white and black plumage, is known as the "*white nun*"'. The female with its chestnut head is known less imaginatively as a "*redhead*". From their summer homes in northern Russia, many thousands spend the winter in the Netherlands and a few hundred come to Britain. In Orkney, where they may be found on any of the county's lowland lochs, there are usually no more than half a dozen records each winter, of which the majority are "*redheads*".

Goosander • *Rantock* • Lochs in autumn, winter and spring; very hard to find

This occasional but yearly visitor to Orkney is very similar to the Red-breasted Merganser but is overall larger. The females bear the most similarities; both are almost identical in shape and colouration, but the Goosander shows a sharp demarcation between the brown head and the magnolia neck, whereas the Red-breasted Merganser's chestnut head-colour merges into the grey neck. There is little trouble in separating the drakes; the Goosander looks generally white and black. The majority of the birds that occur in Orkney appear in the winter months from October to March and have been seen on a variety of inland waters including the Peedie Sea in Kirkwall. Occasionally birds have been seen on burns and lochs on Hoy and Rousay in the summer months, giving rise to

the possibility of breeding. It is a bird of upland rivers and since 1871, when Britain's first breeding Goosanders were discovered in Perthshire, it has increased dramatically.

Ruddy Duck • Lowland lochs, especially Mill Dam, Shapinsay all year; hard to find

This controversial little duck is a North American species that was imported by the Wildfowl Trust to Gloucestershire in 1948. Some birds soon escaped and in the following years, Ruddy Ducks colonized much of Britain becoming particularly numerous in the Midlands of England. In Orkney the first bird was seen in 1980. Seventeen years later a pair bred successfully in Holm. In subsequent years, the Mill Dam RSPB Reserve on Shapinsay has been home to at least two breeding pairs. The male with his chestnut-red plumage and vivid pale blue bill is unmistakable and looks like the archetypal bath-tub duck, especially when he is engaged in his bubbling courtship display.

Goosanders (drake in the left background and duck in the left foreground) and Smews (drake on left and duck on right) in December on the Loch of Wasdale, Firth – background, crannog and conifer-surrounded Wasdale.

Ruddy Ducks (drake and duck, drake in the foreground) in June at the RSPB's Mill Dam reserve, Shapinsay – background, the hide at the Mill Dam RSPB reserve.

Red Grouse • *Muir-hen, Muir Pout* • Moorlands all year; not easy to find

A walk through heather is often enlivened by an explosion of dark brown feathers accompanied by rapid cackling and whirring of wings. Red Grouse are plump, very dark and fly low on bowed wings, alternating between beating and gliding. The hens are slightly paler than the liver-brown cocks. Only found in Britain and Ireland, it is a race of the Willow Grouse that occurs over much of northern Europe and exhibits wholly white wings and an all white

winter plumage. In Orkney, their bones have been recovered from many archaeological sites and historical records indicate they were common throughout the county in the late 17th century, probably occurring on every heather covered island. Reclamation of the hill land has had an obvious impact and nowadays they occur far less widely. They have vanished from Shapinsay and Eday and now occur only on Mainland, Hoy, Rousay, Stronsay, Cava, Fara, Flotta and Gairsay. Red Grouse prefer young heather as food and need older heather for cover; consequently they thrive better on moorland that is managed to produce a patchwork of different-aged heather. They are most abundant on the hills of eastern Scotland and eastern England and on the "Glorious 12th" as many as a million brace are shot in Britain. The tradition is still kept alive in Orkney; Groundwater considered Rousay Red Grouse to be the heaviest of all Scotland.

Pheasant • Grasslands, scrub and cereal stubbles all year; easy to find

These spectacular and noisy game birds have been in Britain for at least one thousand years and for most of that time were restricted to lowland woods bordering arable fields in the south of England. With the rise in popularity of "the shoot", Pheasants were introduced into Scotland in the late 16th century. Early introductions were of the Old English type (*colchicus*), those without a white collar, while since the 18th century most have been of the Ring-necked type (*torquatus*), those with a white collar and originating from China. They are the commonest game bird in Britain and each year the "wild" population is supplemented by 15 million released birds, hand-reared for shooting. By the end of the season (1st October to 1st February) at least 12 million of these birds have been shot. In Orkney, initial introductions during the 19th century at Binscarth and Muddiesdale were unsuccessful. It is only since the 1970s that Pheasants have become established in Orkney. Now they can be found on most of the islands and new agricultural-environment schemes will also benefit Orkney's Pheasants; some set-aside fields can attract as many as fifty birds in autumn and winter. The gaudy cocks are seen at their best in early spring when the dominant birds attract a harem of broody females who may incubate as many as 20 eggs. Females and young birds are brown and alike.

Red Grouse (cock in foreground, hen behind and three chicks) in June on Gairsay – background, the Hen of Gairsay and Shapinsay.

Pheasants (two cocks and three hens) in November at Dale, Costa, Evie – (l-r) Costa Hill and Newton. The cock Ring-necked Pheasant is in the foreground and the cock "Old English" is on the left.

Quail • Grasslands and cereal fields in spring and summer; very hard to find

This, like the Corncrake, Spotted Crake and Water Rail, is a bird that is more likely to be heard than seen. It spends the winter in Africa and appears annually in Orkney in varying numbers; its arrival is probably due to helping southerly winds accompanied by spring droughts in France and Spain. They are at home in cereal fields and have been heard and sometimes seen throughout Orkney; breeding has been proved on a few occasions. In some years there may be just a single record (in 2005, the only instance was of a corpse found at a Merlin's plucking post on Hoy) while in other years there may be a dozen (in 1998, birds were heard on Egilsay, South Ronaldsay, Shapinsay, Papa Westray, Stronsay and Holm). Their call is highly recognisable and is usually written down as "*wet my lips*".

Red-legged Partridge • Grasslands and cereal fields all year, especially on Shapinsay; very hard to find

Two species of partridge have been introduced into Orkney. The Grey Partridge, a native to Britain, has been released on numerous occasions, the first at the end of the 18th century. Since then there have been introductions on Rousay and Shapinsay and in St Andrews plus occasional sightings in the West Mainland. However none have been seen since 1994. In Britain, the Grey Partridge has been declining for at least fifty years; the major cause has been the use of herbicides that have reduced the amount of insect food available to chicks. The Red-legged Partridge was introduced near Kirkwall in 1840 but failed. However, since 2001, following the release of captive hand-reared birds, sightings have occurred most frequently on Shapinsay, but also in St Ola and St Andrews. It may be that with this steady series of sightings, its monotonous song, likened to a labouring steam engine, may be heard more in Orkney. The species was first introduced to England from France in the 17th century; it is also known as the "Frenchman". Where the Grey Partridge has declined, the "Frenchman" seems to have flourished; it is considered hardier than the Grey Partridge, can have a second clutch and is more tolerant of wooded landscapes (they have been seen perched on the garden walls of Balfour Castle).

Quail in June at the Bu, Wyre – (l-r)Point of Avelshay, Rousay, Rousay Sound and Egilsay.

Red-legged Partridges in June at the Hillock of Burroughston Broch, Shapinsay.

Black-throated Diver • Inshore, especially Scapa Flow, in autumn, winter and spring; hard to find

Between the months of September and June Scapa Flow is the most likely locality for this bird. Most sightings are of birds in winter or juvenile dress, but occasionally in spring and early summer a bird in its stunning breeding plumage may be encountered. Superficially they appear more like Great Northern Divers than Red-throated Divers but there are certain characteristics and pointers that set them apart. First of all, the Black-throated Divers in Scapa Flow are usually seen in a fairly tight-knit group of about twenty birds. This flock often appears as a sea-borne line or procession. During springtime, this line will suddenly disappear as the birds engage in underwater display and reappear some 30 seconds later. Secondly, and possibly the most conclusive evidence that you are watching Black-throated Divers, is if you manage to see the white oval mark towards the rear of the bird just above the water line. Some of the best places to search for this diver include Echnaloch Bay, Howequoy Head in Holm, from the Hobbister cliffs, and from the deck of the ferry from Houton to Lyness. As a British breeding bird, the Black-throated Diver is restricted to north and west Scotland where it breeds on larger lochs than the Red-throated Diver – unlike the Red, the Black needs a bigger take-off area. There are in the region of 150 pairs and though Orkney appears to have suitable sites, breeding has never been known. In the winter, peak numbers occur on the west coast of Scotland and the Moray Firth; the latter site is probably attractive to birds from Scandinavia and Russia.

Great Northern Diver • *Immer Goose* • Inshore or at sea in autumn, winter and spring; easy to find

This is an Orkney speciality and can be seen throughout the islands between September and June. They are big birds and the Orkney reference to 'goose' is apt – the "*Immer*" comes from the Icelandic "*himi brimi*" meaning surf-roarer. In the winter months almost any stretch of inshore water supports the Great Northern and on calm winter days, they appear as large and stately birds dotted separately over the sea. They rarely go in for sociability and in the main are loners jealously patrolling their winter-feeding patches. A typical view would be of a headless bird motoring purposefully through the water and emerging with a wriggling fish in its substantial bill. Great Northerns have a characteristic head shape; above the bill a steep-sloped forehead meets a very flat crown. The neck pattern is a distinguishing identification feature; on a Black-throated, the black and white is evenly split in a straight line, while on a Great Northern the black and white meets in indented form. Occasionally birds linger over summer and breeding, though never proved, has been suspected in northwest Scotland. In springtime you may be fortunate to hear their yodelling, wailing and moaning calls which can make the hair on the back of your neck stand up. Orkney's birds probably spend the summer in Iceland, Greenland and Canada and, by the autumn, favoured areas like Scapa Flow and Deer Sound support internationally important numbers. Wintering birds can be found around the coasts of north and west Britain; however no site is as important as Scapa Flow which, in 1998, held 781 birds, a quarter of all the birds spending the winter in Britain.

Black-throated Divers (three in winter plumage) in Scapa Flow during winter – (l-r) Flotta, Flotta oil terminal and Hoy.

Great Northern Divers (summer plumage in foreground and winter plumage behind) during May in the String off the Point of Dishan, Shapinsay – background, the Douche and Balfour Castle.

Red-throated Diver • *Rain Goose, Loom, Loon* • Mainly upland lochs in summer; inshore or at sea in autumn, winter and spring; easy to find

There can be few more stirring sights to see than the courtship display of these magical birds as they wail, yodel, crash and splash in synchronicity on Orkney's lochs and lochans. With over 100 nests in the county, Orkney is one of the best-blessed localities in Britain to see this species that goes by the name of "*loom*" or "*loon*". Judging by the number of lochs called "loomachun", it is evident that the bird was known in Orkney during Viking times. Many of the county's peat lochs have resident loon pairs but Hoy, with an abundance of remote lochans, is home to the majority (one of Hoy's birds is known to be at least 24 years old). However, the largest breeding gatherings are not found on Hoy; this distinction is held by the Mill Loch on Eday and Looma Chun in West Mainland that support anything up to seven pairs each. Red-throated Divers can even be found on some of the larger lowland lochs such as Harray, Kirbister, Hundland and Boardhouse. Listen for the guttural "*kok kok kok*" call which they utter as they return from the sea to greet their partner or feed their offspring. Their breeding range in Britain is restricted to northern and western Scotland where there are about 1400 pairs extending from their stronghold in Shetland south to the Isle of Arran; also, there are a few pairs now nesting in northwest Ireland. While not averse to nesting on the banks and shores of large bodies of water, they tend to favour small hill lochans; they have the ability to take off in shorter spaces than their cousin the Black-throated Diver. After the breeding season, they are more difficult to find in Orkney waters, but there is always the chance of seeing them off any of the Churchill barriers. Many of Orkney's birds head south and they have been found along both the east and west coasts of Britain and Ireland with one bird going as far afield as Lorient in western France. Around Britain, concentrations of Icelandic and Scandinavian Red-throated Divers can be found in the sheltered bays along the east coast. During the winter of 1982, the Moray Firth held over 1500 birds, while off the Suffolk coast in 1999, an abundance of sprats grabbed the attention of at least 2,000 birds. In winter, their plumage is less dramatic and more greyish, but you can often identify them by the manner in which they seem to hold their head and bill in a slightly haughty, head-in-the-air, attitude.

Red-throated Divers (summer plumage) in June nesting at Lowrie's Water, Burgar Hill, Evie – background, RSPB hide and turbines.

Little Grebe • *Little Footy Arse*
• Lowland lochs all year, and inshore waters in winter; not easy to find

On a calm summer's morning a far-carrying whinnying peal of laughter may be heard coming from some of Orkney's lochs. This could very well be your first indication that Little Grebes may be nesting close by. Apart from chicks and ducklings, Little Grebes are just about the smallest bird on a loch – a tail-less ball of fluff that can be infuriatingly difficult to see. They spend much of their time skulking among shoreside vegetation or diving in search of small fish and are rarely in the binoculars for a long time. At other times, however, they may be absorbed in display rituals or feeding youngsters and viewing is a lot easier. Little Grebes prefer lochs with an abundance of luxuriant vegetation both on the bottom and as a dense growth of emergent plants. Not all lochs are suitable, but those that are mean that it occurs as a breeding bird on many of Orkney's larger islands. Some of the most regularly frequented breeding sites include Graemeshall Loch, the Loch of Bosquoy, Echna Loch, Liddle Loch, Bea Loch on Sanday, the Mill Dam on Shapinsay and the Lochs of Burness and Saintear on Westray. It is a widespread bird in lowland Britain with the highest numbers occurring along major river valleys. In winter, Little Grebes are more dispersed and can occur away from regular breeding sites

42

Little Grebes (summer plumage) in May at Loch of
Graemeshall, Holm – background, Graemeshall farm and Graemeshall.

Little Grebe (winter plumage) in December at Brig o'Waithe, Stromness.

Red-necked Grebes (summer plumage left, winter plumage right) during April
in St.Mary's Bay, Holm – background, St Mary's pier and village.

– even frequenting the inshore waters of Scapa Flow. At Voy on the Loch of Stenness, up to five birds can be seen in the winter months, while the Brig o' Waithe has been for a long time a well-frequented haunt by anything up to ten birds. It is probable that any suitable stretch of water may hold Little Grebes; lone individuals have been recorded on the Peedie Sea in Kirkwall, and even in water-filled quarry holes such as those at Stanger Head on Flotta, Uppertown on Hoxa Head and Southtown on Burray. Some of these birds will likely be winter immigrants from Europe.

Red-necked Grebe • Inshore in autumn, winter and spring; very hard to find

Baikie and Heddle whose *Historia Naturalis Orcadensis* was published in 1848 considered that the Red-necked Grebe was not uncommon in Orkney in winter. Subsequent authors and ensuing records indicate that the bird is a rather scarce winter visitor. Individuals tend to be found in shallow inshore waters and the most likely location for them is Scapa Flow. An average year in Orkney will produce just a handful of sightings but occasionally as many as ten birds can be located offshore at the county's most frequented site, the Bay of Sandoyne in Holm. In Britain it spends the winter in sheltered inshore localities on the east and south coasts or on larger inland waters. It's a chunky bird, substantially bigger than either the Little Grebe or the Slavonian Grebe. Winter plumage is essentially black and white, although the neck is grey, quite different to the whiteness of a Slavonian Grebe's neck. Sun and good light should also mean that the colour and shape of the bill is scrutinized; a Red-necked's bill is black and yellow and dagger shaped. Summer sightings in Orkney, when the bird sports a rusty red neck are sporadic and not annual but individuals do occur and are again chiefly seen in Scapa Flow. Red-necked Grebes breed on shallow well-vegetated bodies of water in central Europe from Denmark eastwards to the Black Sea. More recently, over-summering pairs in all the home nations have hinted that these grebes may yet become established in Britain.

Slavonian Grebes (summer plumage left, winter plumage right) during May in Orphir Bay, Orphir – (l-r) Gruf Hill, Ward Hill and Akla with St Nicholas's kirk.

Slavonian Grebe • Inshore and larger lowland lochs in autumn, winter and spring; easy to find

Considering that Orkney is blessed with a moderately large number of Slavonian Grebes and that they can be seen in most months, it's surprising they do not possess an Orkney name. During the winter months they are far more numerous and far easier to see than the Little Grebe which does possess an Orkney label. Scapa Flow alone holds upwards of a hundred birds in winter – such numbers mean that the Flow is of importance both nationally and internationally being home to a third of Britain's, and 2.5% of Europe's wintering populations. Within the Flow, the most favoured sites include Echnaloch Bay, Swanbister Bay in Orphir and on Hoy, Mill Bay and North Bay. At all these locations it's possible to see as many as twenty birds in their loose flocks. Birds can also be located on some of Orkney's larger lochs, with Harray, Stenness, Boardhouse and Tankerness being favoured locations. Most sightings are of birds in winter plumage; at this stage of the year they are simply black and white with the black confined to the upper parts and the cap. They also give the overall impression of being very small and serpent-like. Come April time, Orkney witnesses birds in their stunning summer plumage of black, chestnut and gold. These jewels are no doubt returning to their breeding lochs in Iceland, Scandinavia and Russia. In 1908 a pair nested in northeast Scotland; this area is the species' stronghold in Britain and now supports at least 60 pairs. Displaying pairs on Orkney waters are not uncommon and breeding may yet occur in the county.

Fulmar • *Mallimack* • At sea, cliffs and inshore all year, inland in summer; very easy to find

It is easy to forget that Fulmars are relative newcomers to the islands. Barely one hundred years ago, Orkney's first breeding pair was found on the Hoy cliffs; before that Fulmars were seen in Orkney only on rare occasions. Its rapid expansion is linked to the vast quantity of offal that resulted from the whaling and fishing industry in the North Atlantic during the 19th and 20th centuries. Initially, St Kilda was Britain's only Fulmar colony but in 1878 Shetland was colonized and in 1900 it was the turn of Orkney. Nowadays Fulmars occur around all of Britain's shores. In Orkney, most Fulmars nest on the high cliffs around the coasts, but, they can also be found on inland hamars such as those at Syradale in Firth and on Hoy and Rousay, on the holms in the Harray Loch, in the shelter of stone dykes, on sand dunes, ruined buildings and even on flat ground. In May the nest contains one large white egg

*Fulmars nesting (adults and one chick)
in July at Marwick Head, Birsay
– background, the Kitchener Memorial.*

that by August becomes one large white chick. Fulmars are wide ranging travellers and many of Orkney's birds have been found in the Faeroes, along the North Sea coasts of Norway, Denmark and Germany and even in Canada. One particular young North Ronaldsay Fulmar, ringed on 8th June 1980 was found dead in Newfoundland 25 days later. They are also long-lived; studies have recognised some birds that have reached their fiftieth year.

The following four species are all hard to see. However after a substantial westerly blow, the best chance of seeing any of them is from locations such as Dennis Head on North Ronaldsay, Mull Head on Papa Westray, Noup Head on Westray, the Brough of Birsay in West Mainland, the Point of Ayre in Deerness and Brough on South Ronaldsay, They can even occur in the more sheltered waters of Scapa Flow.

Manx Shearwater • *Lyre, Lyrie* • At sea in spring, summer and autumn; hard to find

The Manx Shearwater was far more common in Orkney than it is now. According to Low (1813), young Manx Shearwaters were salted down and boiled with cabbage by "the country people". Place names such as Lyrawa on Hoy and Lyre Geo near Yesnaby indicate its former presence and the nickname Lyars for folk from Walls suggests Manxies were commonplace there. Rats and cats have no doubt reduced their numbers. Nowadays it may be that just a few pairs breed on Hoy and at times small flocks can be seen in Rackwick on summer evenings. Unlike the all-dark Sooty Shearwater, the Manx Shearwater looks very black and white as it shears and glides low over the waves. The British breeding population is concentrated in a few remote islands off the west coast; there are 150,000 pairs on Rum, the largest colony in the world.

Manx Shearwaters during June at Rack Wick, Hoy – (l-r) Rora Head, Too of the Head, Moor Fea and Clicknafea.

Storm Petrel • *Alamotti, Mootie, Gourder, Storm Finch* • At sea in spring, summer and autumn; hard to find

This tiny all dark bird with a white rump is the smallest and one of the most secretive seabirds nesting in Britain. Most colonies occur on offshore islands to the north and west of Britain. During the breeding season the birds spend the day either far out to sea feeding on plankton or in their nest chambers located in a rabbit burrow, stone dyke or boulder beach and up to a metre below ground. At night the birds come ashore to swap incubating duties with their partner or to feed their youngsters. Historical records indicate that they bred on many of the uninhabited islands; nowadays the main colonies can be found on Auskerry, Rusk Holm, Swona, Sule Skerry and the Holm of Papay. It may be that they still breed in substantial numbers, but like the Manx Shearwater, rats may have played a significant part in their current distribution. They are exceptionally nomadic and through ringing many of Orkney's Storm Petrels are known to frequent other British colonies and have been found in the Faeroes, Norway, France, Portugal, Namibia and South Africa. Their oceanic wanderings are well portayed by one individual that was caught and ringed on North Ronaldsay on 22nd July 2000, recaught in Rogaland, Norway on 25th July and subsequently recaught near Aberdeen on 30th July. Unlike the Leach's Petrel, it shows white on the underside of the wing.

Sooty Shearwater • At sea in autumn; hard to find

The Sooty Shearwater is one of the world's great ocean travellers. They nest in the southern hemisphere and the nearest colony to Orkney is in southern Argentina. Despite this huge distance, Sooty Shearwaters pass the Orkney coast each year, and in some years pass it in quite considerable numbers. In late summer and early autumn look out for a dark cigar-shaped-bodied and narrow-winged bird shearing and scything through the air and skimming over the waves.

Leach's Petrel • At sea in autumn; very hard to find

This is another ocean wanderer and as with others of its type, there is still a great deal to be discovered about it. Just like the Storm Petrel, it spends daylight hours out at sea and returns to its burrow under cover of night. There is a general feeling that Leach's Petrels may breed in Orkney but this is based solely on a 1933 record from Sule Skerry and the fact that occasionally Leach's are caught and ringed in the summer months. Although superficially similar to a Storm Petrel it is slightly larger, has a pale 'W' on its wings and flies over the sea in a more purposeful manner.

*Storm Petrels in July
off Auskerry lighthouse.*

*Sooty Shearwaters and Leach's Petrel
in October in the Bay of Sjaevar, North Ronaldsay
– background, the Old Beacon at Dennis Head.*

51

Gannets nesting (adults and one chick) in June on the Noup cliffs, Westray – background, Haas of the Stack and Noup lighthouse. A third year bird is flying.

Gannet • *Sula, Solan Goose* • At sea and inshore in spring, summer and autumn; easy to find

It takes up to six years for a Gannet to attain its adult plumage. Once reached, its brilliant white and black plumage is topped off with a yellow/orange head and a pale blue bill. In the years leading up to plumage maturity, it develops from an all dark juvenile through different stages of dark and light and with each successive year, the amount of white increases as the black/brown decreases. Whatever they are doing, Gannets are spectacular to watch. Fishing birds arrow into the sea in pursuit of their prey – listen out for the accompanying splash. Flying birds ooze majesty as they power their way, often in formation, to and from their breeding colonies. Within Britain and Ireland there are just two dozen gannetries and these colonies hold almost three quarters of the world's Gannets. Most colonies occur on islands in the north and west of Britain where birds are close to their food supplies of herring, mackerel and sand eels and where cliffs provide updraughts and currents for take offs and landings. In Orkney, there are about 5,000 pairs on Sule Stack and this colony has been in existence for at least 400 years. Apart from a couple of isolated breeding attempts on Copinsay in the late 18th and early 19th centuries, Sule Stack was the county's only colony until birds decided to breed at the Noup Head on Westray and at Sule Skerry in 2003. Both these small colonies are increasing annually. It is evident that birds from

Shags in March on Point of Oxan, Graemsay-background, Hoy Low.

other British colonies come to Orkney either to fish or to seek breeding opportunities. A young bird ringed on the Bass Rock, Lothian in 1974 was found dead on Hunda in the spring of 1986 and another young bird, this time ringed on Ailsa Craig in 1963 expired in Stenness in 1986. They are also fairly long lived, a prime example being the 37-year-old bird from the Bass Rock that was found dead in Herston in 1998. After the breeding season, many of Orkney's birds head south to winter off the French and Portuguese coasts.

Shag • *Scarf, Tappie Whaesie* • At sea and inshore all year; very easy to find

This is one of the most commonly seen birds in Orkney and a coastal walk without seeing a Shag would be an extremely rare occurrence. They are abundant and widespread throughout the year and their commonness is indicated by the many places that include "*scarf*" or "*scarva*" in their name. During the Second World War Shags were caught in considerable numbers and sent south to restaurants. Cormorants and Shags look alike but Shags are substantially smaller, are green-black and often have a short erect crest. They are strictly coastal and, unlike Cormorants, seldom feed on inland waters. While on the water, Shags generally leap into the water in pursuit of their prey. They prefer deep water where they can catch sand eels, and rocky coasts where they can nest on ledges, in caves or boulder beaches. Scapa Flow supports nationally important numbers. Almost 10% of Britain's wintering population remain here and large numbers can be found congregating around Graemsay, Clestrain in Stenness, Switha and Bring Head on Hoy. As breeding birds they are chiefly found on Britain's west coast and from ringing studies, it seems apparent that during the winter, many Shags move into Orkney from Shetland, northeast Scotland and the Firth of Forth. Ringing also illustrates that some Orkney birds move south; during the winter of 1984, a young bird from South Ronaldsay was found dead off the Essex coast and an intriguing item involved a young bird hatched on Sule Skerry in 1982 and nine years later was found breeding on Craigleith Island in Lothian.

Cormorant • *Great Scarf, Hibling, Lerblade, Palmer* • Inshore and lowland lochs all year; easy to find

These large reptilian looking birds are not uncommon but nowhere near as common as their cousin the Shag with which there is often the possibility of confusion. However, familiarity with their differences in appearance and habits makes separation a lot easier. Cormorants are a lot bigger than Shags. They tend to be blacker, have a white chin and cheeks and in spring sport a large white patch on their thighs. The bills, which can be bright yellow, are much heavier looking. Unlike Shags, Cormorants can be found inland and lochs such as Harray and Stenness are frequent haunts. They fly overland (something a Shag very rarely does) and they can often be seen high above Binscarth Wood flying to and from Wide Firth. Young Cormorants usually show a large amount of paleness on their bellies. Cormorants are colonial nesters and current colonies include the Calf of Eday, Holm of Boray, Little Green Holm, Seal Skerry and the Brough on Stronsay. The Calf of Eday is the largest colony and supports almost 150 nests. In Britain they breed mainly on the west coast and occasionally inland in trees. During the winter, ringing recoveries indicate that some of Orkney's Cormorants range along both the North Sea and Irish Sea coasts and occasionally even enter the English Channel. Conversely, birds from Norway and Denmark are known to visit the county in winter.

Grey Heron • *Hegrie, Skiop Herie* • Inshore and lowland lochs all year; easy to find

In Britain, except for mountainous areas, breeding birds are widespread and most heronries occur in trees. However where trees are absent, Grey Herons are able to utilise low bushes, heather and cliffs. As a breeding bird the Grey Heron has never been numerous in Orkney and has become less so. A small colony of up to 13 nests existed on the cliffs near Yesnaby from 1863 until 1979, and a similar sized colony, established in the pines of the Lyrawa plantation on Hoy during the 1980s, has been lost. Previously Grey Herons had nested on Glimps Holm, Black Craig near Stromness and Rothiesholm on Stronsay. During late summer and autumn, birds from mainland Scotland, Denmark, Norway and Sweden arrive in Orkney and winter feeding patches are jealously guarded. Feeding territories include shallow coastal water and shallow inland lochs, burns and ditches. Grey Herons roost together and some of the most favoured sites such as the Ouse in Finstown, the Loch of Tankerness, the Loch of Graemeshall in Holm and Skaill on Eday may have as many as twenty birds.

Left: Cormorants at their nests in June on the Calf of Eday, Eday – (l-r) Carrick House, Calf Sound and Red Head.

Grey Herons in September at Bore of Vigga, Holm – (l-r) Westersand, St Nicholas kirk and Roseness.

55

White-tailed Eagle • *Erne* • Coasts and uplands in spring; very hard to find

These magnificent raptors, which feed on fish, hares, rabbits, seabirds and carrion, once occupied many sites throughout Orkney as they did throughout wilder Britain. Its one-time presence in Orkney is celebrated in many place names – Ernie Tooin in Rendall, Erne Toog in Stromness and Erne Tower on Rousay. In the 17th century Sibbald considered that their "many breeding places" included the east side of Mainland as well as Hoy. They were deemed to be a pest of the highest order – the Kirkwall Act offered eight pence for a slain bird and a staggering 20 shillings for each robbed egg. Two centuries later, authors indicated nesting sites at Mull Head in Deerness, Ernie Tower on Costa Hill in Birsay, Hoy, South Ronaldsay, Switha and Eday. Its potential threat to lambs led to its persecution and disappearance; the last breeding in Orkney occurred in 1873, Shetland's last bird was shot in 1917 and Scotland's last eyrie was located in Skye in 1916. There have been three attempts to reintroduce the White-tailed Eagle to Britain; the first was in 1959 in Argyll and the second on Fair Isle in 1968. Only seven birds were involved and both attempts proved unsuccessful. In 1975 a much bigger project was initiated; based on the island of Rum it involved the release of 82 Norwegian birds in the subsequent ten years. Thirty years later, the Scottish population numbers thirty pairs and is now self-sustaining. Birds, though always rare, are seen in Orkney annually, usually in spring. How long will it be before they nest again in the county? Look out for a "flying door" – broad rectangular fingered wings and a short wedge-shaped tail.

White-tailed Eagles in April near Geo of the Light, Stourdale, Hoy – background, the Old Man of Hoy and M.V. Hamnavoe.

Marsh Harrier

• Lowland lochs and wetlands in spring, summer and autumn; hard to find

During the 1950s and 1960s, Marsh Harrier numbers had declined quite dramatically over much of northern Europe. In Britain, the population had been reduced to just one pair by 1971, and this one pair became the main attraction at Minsmere RSPB reserve in Suffolk. The evidence strongly suggested that the decline was due to environmental contaminants such as organochlorine pesticides. Since the withdrawal of these compounds, the Marsh Harrier population has made a remarkable recovery. In England its stronghold is East Anglia with outliers in Somerset, Kent, Lancashire and the Humber. Reed beds in Scotland have also proved attractive and breeding birds can be found along the River Tay. Orkney too, has benefited from the resurgence of Marsh Harriers. From a position of being an occasional visitor, Marsh Harriers became frequent spring visitors in the 1980s and 1990s and since then have even started to breed in two or three of Orkney's prime wetland sites. Any harrier quartering a wetland area is worth a second look – it may be a Marsh Harrier! Unlike Hen Harriers, Marsh Harriers do not have a white rump. The female is an all-dark bird with a pale crown and shoulders. The male appears three-coloured with black fingered wings and a dark mantle that contrasts with grey wings and tail.

Marsh Harriers (male in the foreground, female behind) in May at Durkadale, Birsay – (l-r) Durkadale farm, Dee of Durkadale and Greeny Hill.

Hen Harrier • *Gos-haak, Kattabelly, Kattakally*
• Moorlands, wetlands, rough grasslands and set-aside all year; easy to find

Breeding birds are found on moorlands over much of Scotland and Orkney ranks as one of the most important places in Britain and Europe for Hen Harriers. During the 19th century, naturalists considered it to have been "one of our most common hawks". However by 1914, and in line with much of the rest of the United Kingdom, the Orkney population had declined to just two pairs mainly due to the activities of nest hunters and egg collectors. Thankfully, in subsequent years, enlightened Orkney naturalists such as George Arthur, Duncan Robertson and Eddie Balfour promoted the Hen Harrier's cause and by the 1970s there were as many as 85 nests. The Orkney population was blessed by having a plentiful supply of Orkney voles, skylarks, meadow pipits, rabbits and wader chicks to prey upon and by the fact that there were no sporting interests to conflict with. In addition, the prime areas chosen for nesting included uplands in the West Mainland, Hoy and Rousay and many of these areas became protected by national designation or RSPB reserve status. There are many more females than males and polygyny is widespread with some males having a harem of up to four females. In autumn and winter communal roosting by as many as twenty birds can be observed in a few favoured sites. More recently however, Hen Harrier numbers have declined and concerted efforts have been made through land management to provide more hunting opportunities and more prey. Ringing has demonstrated that many birds head south for the winter and individuals have been seen as far away as Northamptonshire, Pembrokeshire and Somerset. Research has also shown that there have been at least two occasions when birds born in Perthshire have travelled north to Orkney to breed. The strangest occurrence however involved an Orkney-born bird that nested in the West Mainland between 1975 and 1981 and in 1984 was discovered breeding near Strontian in the western Highlands. Unlike the Marsh Harrier, both the male and female have white rumps. The brown female Hen Harrier is appreciably larger than the grey male. Both can be seen hunting low over rough grassland or crops during the winter while in spring there are few more thrilling sights than skydancing courting harriers.

Hen Harriers (male in the background, female in front) skydancing in April over Sleet Moss, Birsay – (l-r) Peerie Water, Rousay and Burgar Hill turbines.

Hen Harriers (male in the foreground, female behind) during November hunting in St. Andrews – background, the Old School House and St. Andrews kirk.

Buzzards in March at Nowt Bield, Hoy.

Buzzard • *Gled* • Woodlands and open country all year; not easy to find

The A9 road journey to Orkney is frequently enlivened by the sight of a perched and motionless Buzzard in a roadside tree or on a fence post or a pair displaying or soaring over their territory. In Britain, it was once a widespread bird but suffered huge persecution in the 18th, 19th and 20th centuries. There was an increase after 1914 when most gamekeepers left the estates to fight for King and country but the Buzzard's good fortunes were short-lived – the introduction of myxomatosis meant that rabbits, their chief food source, were suddenly off the menu and organochlorine pesticides left their deathly mark, as they did for many other raptors. However, as with other birds of prey, their fortunes have taken a turn for the better and they are now found widely, mainly in the western half of Britain. Apparently it has always been a rare bird in Orkney although the excavation of chambered tombs at Midhowe on Rousay and Quanterness in the West Mainland yielded Buzzard bones. During the 1960s a pair took up residence on Hoy and by mid decade there were two pairs. Nowadays it is considered that up to three pairs nest on Hoy. Individuals have been seen in the Firth and Rendall area for the last ten years and nesting may have occurred in 2005. Binscarth wood is a favourite site for them, and birds are frequently seen on Rousay. During autumn, migrant birds may be encountered on any coast. Buzzards are predominantly dark brown but their plumage can be highly variable.

Sparrowhawk • Woodlands, gardens, towns and open country all year; not easy to find

Each evening, as the black flocks of Starlings gather over Kirkwall in autumn and winter before dropping down to roost

Sparrowhawks
(male on the left, female on right) in spring at Woodwick, Evie.

in the town's sycamores, you can almost guarantee seeing a Sparrowhawk causing consternation among the flying ranks. The ensuing aerial display can be spectacular as the Starlings endeavour to elude the aggressor – the shape of the flock ever-changing in a constant swirl and sweep of flight. Sparrowhawks have never been common nesters in Orkney; their favoured breeding sites are coniferous plantations and amenity woodlands. However, Hoy has a few conifer plantations, and amenity woodlands occur in the East and West Mainland, on Rousay and Shapinsay, so there is enough suitable habitat for at least a dozen pairs. A feature of the last twenty years has been increased tree planting and it may be that more Sparrowhawks will nest in the county. Like many British birds of prey, the Sparrowhawk has suffered not only from human persecution, but also from the use of organochlorine pesticides and during the 1950s its fortunes were bleak. Limited persecution still continues but the threat from pesticides has been removed. It now occurs over much of Britain although is not found on the highest ground or in the Outer Hebrides. Scandinavian birds are frequently caught at North Ronaldsay Bird Observatory in the autumn and ringing has indicated that many of them go on to spend winter much further south – indeed one bird was subsequently retrapped in the French Pyrenees. The male is smaller than the female and is seen less frequently. This is probably because being smaller and more manoeuvrable he can hunt for songbirds in the woodlands, whereas the larger female prefers to hunt over open country. The male is slate grey with a rusty red wash on the flanks and cheeks. Females are grey brown while young birds are brown. In flight look out for their short, rounded and bulging wings.

Golden Eagle • *Ainie-onyoo* • Uplands all year; very hard to find

There are little more than 400 pairs of Golden Eagles in Britain. Of those, one pair is in England and the rest are in Scotland and it is a great pity that Orkney does not feature in the figures any more. These magnificent birds can be found in the remote hills and glens of northwest Britain. They nest on crags or in ancient Scots Pines and feed on Red Grouse and Mountain Hare. Apart from the Scots Pines, the other requirements all occur on Hoy and in the 19th century one pair bred there, using eyries either at the Sneuk, Meadow of the Kame or the Dwarfie Hamars. By the end of the century, the Hoy skies had lost their Golden Eagles. Persecution may have played its part; one Orkney author (Rev. G.Barry, 1805) maintained "it did great devastation among poultry, pigs, sheep and lambs". Surprisingly though, this was not the end of Golden Eagles on Hoy; in 1966 a pair returned, bred successfully on 11 occasions, but by 1982 had departed. Wandering individuals are seen almost annually in Orkney and it's to be hoped they'll once again grace the skies of Hoy daily.

Golden Eagles (and Mountain Hare) in February at Dwarfie Stane and Dwarfie Hamars, Hoy.

Osprey • Coasts and lochs in spring; very hard to find

Most visiting Ospreys are seen in Orkney during May or June. These are probably young birds that have travelled too far north from the core Scottish population or have been blown off course en route to their Scandinavian breeding sites as they journey back from West Africa. Birds have been seen in a variety of locations, some flying over the hill pursued by irate nesting gulls or Ravens, others seen catching fish from inland lochs and inshore waters. Sometimes they can be mistaken for a large immature gull – so take a second look! The Osprey is one of Britain's best-known success stories. It became extinct in 1916 but returned to breed at Loch Garten in 1955. Since then the species has flourished in Scotland in line with an upsurge in the Scandinavian population. Now birds breed widely throughout the east and central areas of the Highlands and the Osprey has even re-established itself in England. However, during its migration the species still suffers at the hands of hunters.

Osprey in June fishing at the Oyce of Rennibister, Firth – (l-r) Rennibister house and Rennibister cottage.

65

Kestrel • *Moosie Haak, Wind Cuffer* • Uplands, cliffs, rough grasslands and open country all year; easy to find

As with all other British birds of prey, the Kestrel has suffered from human persecution and from the use of organochlorine pesticides. During the 1950s, its population in Britain was at its leanest. In these more enlightened times, the Kestrel is a numerous and widespread raptor nesting in a wide variety of habitats that include woods, sea cliffs, moorland, parks and cities. In addition its increased familiarity is due to the frequency with which we see Kestrels hovering over motorways and for the fact that its hovering form is the logo for the RSPB's Young Ornithologists Club. In days past, most Orkney crofts had cereal stacks in their yards from autumn to spring. Finches and mice found sustenance from the spilt grain during the hardest times of the year and each cereal stack seemed to have its own Kestrel or "Moosie Haak" in residence. This was a time of plenty for Kestrels and it was considered to be Orkney's commonest hawk. It has been recorded nesting in a variety of sites in Orkney – these have included quarry faces, sea cliffs, old mills and kirks. Indeed, during the 19th century a pair nested for many years on St Magnus Cathedral. Because of the lack of ground predators in Orkney, Kestrels have also been known to nest in heather although, as with other ground nesting birds, they are susceptible to the attentions of feral cats. Kestrels are no longer as common as they were formerly. In the 1950s there may have been as many as 20 pairs. Nowadays there are few farms with cereal stacks and the number of breeding Kestrels in Orkney may amount to no more than ten pairs. In the autumn Swedish and Finnish birds have been found in the county while some Orkney-born birds have been known to spend winter in Somerset and Devon. The males are distinguished from females and young birds by the blue grey head, blue grey tail and black tail band.

Kestrels (male hovering, female perched) in April at Lamb Holm – (l-r) Burray, Weddell Sound, Glimps Holm and No 2 barrier.

Merlins (male flying, female perched) in April at Cottascarth, Rendall – (l-r) Eddie Balfour hide, Enyas Hill, Dale.

Merlin • *Smyril* • Moorlands, coasts, rough grasslands and open country all year; not easy to find

In winter Orkney's upland areas can appear harsh and hostile. During the fullness of summer, Meadow Pipits and Skylarks will have raised broods on the hill's wealth. But as this wealth declines and the weather deteriorates, there is an exodus of these birds to lower ground – coastal farmland and the shore. The Merlins will follow their prey and it is at this time that these dashing raptors can be encountered perched on roadside fences, either digesting their last meal or on the lookout for their next. This, the smallest of Britain's raptors, nests almost exclusively in open upland areas dominated by heather. Elsewhere in the northern hemisphere, the Merlin is more typically a bird of forest margins and there has been a recent tendency for British birds to follow suit. In Orkney, nesting Merlins are confined to the hill land of Hoy, West Mainland, Rousay and occasionally Eday and Stronsay where they nest on slopes of long heather. Merlins are difficult birds to see on their breeding territory but the RSPB's Eddie Balfour hide in the amphitheatre of Cottascarth in Rendall provides the best opportunity in the county. Like all other birds of prey nationally, the

Merlin has suffered the twin blows of persecution and pesticide contamination. In Orkney persecution is unheard of but a decrease in breeding numbers and the discovery of thin eggshells in the 1970s indicated organochlorine. There may have been at least 25 pairs of Merlins in Orkney before 1960; nowadays there is probably three quarters that number. Through ringing, it is known that birds born in Shetland and the north of Scotland, have in subsequent years, taken up territory in Orkney. One particular far-travelling youngster that was born in the county in 1990 was found a year later in Navarra, Spain some 1800km distant. The blue males are a good deal smaller than the brown females. In medieval times, the male was known as the ladies' falcon.

Peregrine • Uplands, coasts and cliffs all year; not easy to find

During the Second World War Peregrines posed a threat to Britain's war effort. With a fancy for members of the pigeon family, the Peregrine unfortunately did not differentiate between Rock Doves, Feral Pigeons and carrier Pigeons. Consequently, the nation's security could have been compromised; the Destruction of Peregrine Falcon Order was issued in 1940 and at least 600 Peregrines were eliminated. Contrast this with its status in medieval times; then the Peregrine was the most prized falcon. Such was its standing that in Scotland legislation to preserve these 'hawks' was put in place in the 12th century and in 1621 the fine for stealing a Peregrine was a sobering £100. Like other raptors, the Peregrine experienced a very low period during the 1950s and 1960s as a result of a cocktail of pesticides. However since then, the Peregrine has fought back strongly and it is considered that there are as many now as there were in the 12th century. Nests are usually on high inland crags, sea cliffs, quarry faces and more recently even high-rise blocks in towns. Some sites have been used for hundreds of years and it's likely that is true for Orkney. About fifteen pairs of Peregrines nest in the county and eyries can be found on the Mainland, Hoy, Rousay, Stronsay, Eday and some of the smaller offshore islands. As with Merlins, results from ringing illustrate that birds born in Shetland and the north of Scotland have subsequently nested in Orkney. They are very noisy birds and their commotion often draws attention to their nest location. The males and females are similarly coloured but the male is almost a third smaller.

Peregrines (male flying, female perched) in April at Starabir, Hobbister, Orphir – background, Roo Point and west Holm cliffs. The male is pursuing a Rock Dove.

Water Rail • Lowland wetlands all year; very hard to find

This, one of the most elusive, eccentric and skulking of birds, usually inhabits dense aquatic vegetation. Its body is well adapted to slipping between the reed stems as are its long-toed feet to supporting it on soft mud or floating leaves. Its mix of browns, greys and buffs, is perfect camouflage and its movements seem considered and premeditated. In summer, breeding Water Rails draw attention to themselves by pig-like squealing cries known as "sharming", but such advertisement of their presence is much less common in winter. Only when conditions are really hard, when frozen mud and water force the Water Rails to seek food outside the shelter of their protective vegetation, are they likely to be seen. Water Rails may be increasing in Orkney. "Sharming" has been heard at a number of appropriate sites throughout the islands during May and June including the Loons RSPB reserve, the Loch of Banks, Mill Dam RSPB reserve on Shapinsay and Graemeshall Loch in Holm. They can be found in wetland over much of lowland Britain.

Spotted Crake • Lowland wetlands in spring and summer; very hard to find

This elusive bird must rank as one of the most difficult to see and one of the most poorly known. Usually the only indication of its presence is its distinctive whiplash call that is mostly offered at night. Historical records indicate that it was a fairly common species in Britain until the mid 19th century but drainage and loss of habitat caused a contraction of its range. Wetland areas with tangles of vegetation, most often willows, seem to be the species' favourite type of site. In Orkney it probably occurs in low numbers every year at typical sites and has been recorded from Sanday, Stronsay, North Ronaldsay, Egilsay and Birsay.

Water Rail in winter at the Orkney brewery, Quoyloo, Sandwick.

Spotted Crake in May at Manse Loch, Egilsay – (l-r) Kierfea hill, Filly Ha' and St Magnus kirk.

Corncrake calling in June at Nouster, Papa Westray – background, St Ann's kirk and the Manse.

Corncrake • Grasslands, hay fields, silage and wetlands in spring and summer; very hard to find

It used to be such a common bird, not only in Orkney but also throughout lowland Britain. Its demise commenced in the 19th century and has been laid firmly at the feet of increased farm mechanization and early cutting of crops. Additionally it is susceptible to overhead power lines and on migration to South Africa is frequently caught in nets set for Quail. At present in Orkney when there are barely 20 calling birds each year, it is difficult to realize how common it once was. In 1969 there were 18 males on Graemsay alone including five nests in one field. Birds also bred on the remotest of islands; Copinsay had breeding birds as did tiny Muckle Skerry in the Pentland Firth. Nationally there has been a slow upturn in its fortunes; thanks to Corncrake schemes which combine late cutting with friendly cutting, there are now over a 1,000 calling males, most of which occur in northwest Scotland. Orkney has yet to recover in the same manner but the right habitat awaits and hopefully we can look forward to the time when folk are kept awake at night by the insistent "*crek crek*" – a call that can be uttered by an individual male 20,000 times in six hours.

Moorhen • *Water-hen* • Lowland wetlands in spring and summer; very hard to find

In Orkney, its distribution is wide and it can be found on any piece of freshwater on most islands – sixty pairs are considered to nest on North Ronaldsay. As with other water birds, it may have been more common than it is at present – drainage of wetlands and the resulting loss of habitat will have affected numbers. Orkney birds appear to be sedentary and in winter the county's breeding population is supplemented by migrants from Europe; birds originating from Holland and Denmark have been found in Orkney during this period. Some favoured locations hold birds in quite large numbers; almost 100 birds were at the Bu on Burray during the winter of 1999, no doubt attracted to the feed put out for the resident farm ducks. Adults are smoky black and sport a red frontal shield and a red and yellow bill; youngsters are brown without the bold head colours. Both show their white flicking scut as they move. It breeds commonly over much of lowland Britain.

Coot • *Snaith, Snysen, Snythe* • Lowland lochs all year; easy to find

Superficially similar to the Moorhen, the Coot is slightly larger, has a white frontal shield on its head and is more likely to be seen in open water. It prefers lochs with submerged and emergent vegetation although in winter it may be found feeding on grassland. An aggressive and quarrelsome bird, fights between territorial males can be spectacular. Supine-lying males kick and grasp with their multi-coloured and many-lobed feet. It breeds on lowland lochs on all the major islands, with the possible exception of Hoy. Orkney's Coots are augmented by European immigrants and during autumn and winter a flock approaching 1,000 birds is annually seen on the Loch of Harray. Like the Moorhen, it breeds commonly over much of lowland Britain.

Moorhen during winter near Maesquoy, Netherbrough, Harray

Coots (two adults and three chicks) in May on Bride's Loch, North Ronaldsay

Oystercatcher • *Skeldro, Scottie, Chaldro, Shaalder* • Coasts and short grasslands; very easy to find

Black and white, with long red legs and red bill, they are unmistakable and have probably been a familiar sight in Orkney for hundreds of years. They are blessed with numerous Orkney names and bone remains have been identified from many of the county's archaeological sites. Oystercatchers in Britain increased in the 20th century when they began nesting inland on cultivated fields and hill ground. They are very liberal in their choice of nest site; most typically they include locations such as sand and shingle beaches and loch shores. However, stranger choices have included the top of stone dykes, the roof of a building and the verge next to the Kirkwall to Stromness road. Oystercatcher behaviour can enhance any walk along the beach; noisy communal piping displays occur prior to nesting; furtive skulking occurs when the parent birds are incubating eggs and kamikaze flying towards the "predator" occurs when their youngsters have emerged. After the breeding season, flocks of Oystercatchers are often found searching for food in newly cut silage fields. Young birds wear their white half collars and adults start to develop their white-collar winter-plumage. Though a few birds remain in Orkney over winter, prolonged icy and frosty weather usually triggers Oystercatcher

Oystercatchers in winter at the southern end of the Loch of Stenness, Stromness – (l-r) Diamond Cottage, Bridgend, the Golden Slipper and Brig o' Waithe.

emigration. Ringing reveals that most of Orkney's birds spend winter in southwest England, southwest Wales, southwest Ireland and northern France. An example of their travels is indicated by a 1977 chick from Papa Westray that was recaught in Cornwall in August 1978 and shot in northern coastal France in November 1987 while an example of their winter loyalties is demonstrated by a 1993 North Ronaldsay chick that was recaught at the same site in north Wales in January 1997, November 1999 and November 2003. Apart from the Moray Firth, the east coasts of Scotland and England are less favoured; a few birds are known to spend winter on the Firth of Forth and the Wash and a youngster, born in Sandwick in 1979, was found in the Netherlands in 1996. A return to milder conditions in late February is often accompanied by a mass overnight arrival of Oystercatchers.

Lapwing • *Teeick, Teeo, Peewit* • Soft coasts and short grasslands; very easy to find

Familiar to most people the Lapwing, like the Oystercatcher, has been the recipient of many different Orkney names. Like the Oystercatcher it is also pied; however the pied plumage is simply a convenient impression from a distance; looked at closely the Lapwing exhibits a splendid array of colours that include greens, blues, browns and maroons on the mantle and vivid chestnut on the underside of the tail. Both sexes have crests; the male's crest is longer than the female's. Lapwings can be seen throughout Orkney and encountered throughout the year. In springtime damp rushy pasture and ploughed fields are alive with the plaintive call and aerial acrobatics of Lapwing pairs. In addition, they can be found breeding on low moorland as long as cultivation is close by. Breeding Lapwing numbers have fallen over the last fifty years due to drainage of the land and a change in agricultural practices such as the increase in autumn sown crops. Lapwing flocks

begin to assemble in June; by July and August the flocks have reached substantial numbers and can be found feeding on newly cut silage fields. Youngsters can travel substantial distances in their first year and Orkney-born birds have been found in western France, Portugal and one from Birsay was found in Pisa, Italy, nine months after hatching. Lured to Orkney by the prospect of mild winters and damp fields packed with grubs, autumn sees the arrival of Lapwing flocks from the Continent and from Scotland. These flocks will remain in Orkney throughout the winter if mild conditions persist, but with the snow and ice imminent, emigration, some of it to Ireland, usually precedes the bad weather.

Lapwings in May near St Magnus kirk, Egilsay
– background, Knitchen Hill, Rousay.

Golden Plover • *Hill Laverock, Plever Pliver* • Short grasslands and soft coasts in winter; easy to find. Moorlands in summer; hard to find

These gentle-eyed waders with their mournful calls are probably more familiar in winter than they are in summer. Their summer plumage is spectacularly gaudy, their winter plumage is much more sombre. In Orkney during the 20th century substantial tracts of hill land were ploughed out and this change has had a marked impact upon the breeding fortunes of the Golden Plover. Even at the end of the 19th century, early writers of natural history suggested land reclamation as one of the causes for a decline in the breeding population. Nowadays Orkney's breeding Golden Plovers can only be found in areas that support extensive hill land such as Hoy, the West Mainland, Rousay and Eday. During September and October, many fields throughout Orkney support large flocks (as many as 2,000) of Golden Plovers that have arrived from Scandinavia, Russia and Iceland. A roosting flock is still and compact; a feeding flock is restless and widespread with individual birds scampering a few steps, listening and then pecking. Disturbed, the flock takes to the air in tight formations before spreading out into loose v-formations at higher altitudes. Often looking decidedly brown and dull, sharp winter sunshine reveals their golden-spangled plumage. A feature of spring is the appearance of summer-plumaged birds roosting in the same field year after year. Some of these birds are of the much darker Northern race.

Golden Plovers in winter at Netherstove, Sandwick – (l-r) Bay of Skaill, Hole o'Row and St Peter's kirk.

Golden Plovers nesting in June on Muckle Bilia Fiold, Evie – background, Burgar Hill and turbines.

Ringed Plovers (male left, two chicks, female right) in May on Nousty Sand, Rousay – (l-r) Saviskaill, Erne Tower and Saviskaill Head.

Ringed Plover • *Sandy Lark, Sandy Laverock, Sinloo* • Soft coasts especially sand and shingle and occasionally inland; easy to find

Almost any sandy or small-pebbled beach in Orkney has a resident pair of Ringed Plovers. Their soft and plaintive rising whistle gives their presence away but often not their position. It takes a stop-start dash across the smooth or pebble-dashed sand for the observer to finally see the bird and once seen, a smile is guaranteed from behind the binoculars. They are plump, round and neat; the "ringed" relates to the black collar which in the male is thicker than that of the female or youngster. During the 20th century, Ringed Plovers have become a victim of our growing passion for seaside recreation – a desirable beach for a pair of Ringed Plovers is equally desirable for human leisure activities. An innocent stroll along the sand during May and June will precipitate an anxious period for the parents, culminating in the familiar broken-wing distraction display. The Outer Hebrides, Shetland and Orkney are important for Ringed Plovers with 40% of the British population breeding there. Nationally, there has been a tendency of late for birds to nest inland, possibly as a consequence of increasing coastal disturbance; even in Orkney, nests can be found on bare stony tracks or ploughed land well away from the sea. Outside the breeding season flocks of up to 100 birds may be located at suitable sites such as Warebeth beach in Stromness.

Grey Plovers (summer plumage in foreground, winter plumage right) in April on Sanday – (l-r) Ayre Sound, Start Point and lighthouse.

Grey Plover • Soft coasts especially sand and shingle in autumn, winter and spring; very hard to find

Superficially in winter the Grey Plover and the Golden Plover can look very alike; both are slender and almost elegant. However, the winter Golden Plover is almost wholly a bird of farmland, while the winter Grey Plover is almost exclusively found at the coast. In terms of abundance they differ considerably; the Golden Plover can be found in Orkney in its thousands, the Grey Plover, in some years, barely gets into double figures. They feed almost exclusively on mud and sand flats, a habitat that is abundant around the coastline of Sanday. Many of Orkney's Grey Plovers gravitate to these feeding grounds during autumn, winter and spring and it is not surprising that the largest flocks, occasionally peaking at 100, have occurred on Sanday. Elsewhere, places to look for them include Deer Sound, Widewall Bay, and any of the sandy and muddy bays on Stronsay, Westray and Papa Westray. While feeding, Grey Plovers tend to be solitary and space themselves at distance from others; when roosting they join with other waders. During spring and autumn, it is possible to see Grey Plovers in their spectacular breeding plumage – this summer dress explains their North American name "Black-bellied Plover". In flight, look out for their characteristic black armpits and white rump.

It's often said that the Knot is best recognised by its lack of striking features. It doesn't have the black belly of a summer Dunlin, the striking whiteness of a winter Sanderling or the bright legs of a Redshank. Its most distinctive feature is its lack of distinction. However this perception does it a great disservice. Although never very numerous, groups of up to 100 birds can be found on Orkney's mudflats in winter. They go about their feeding in a considered and careful way and are usually gregarious, either mixing with their own or with other waders in their pursuit of sand worms and small crustaceans. They are bigger than Dunlin and smaller than Redshank; essentially they are a dumpy, pot-bellied and pearl-grey wader with a black bill and black legs. Orkney's small groups of Knot spend the winter on mudflats such as at Widewall Bay on South Ronaldsay, Sandisand in Deerness and Mill Sands in St Andrews, having arrived after a summer spent in Canada and Greenland. During their three months in the high Arctic, they are almost unrecognisable as the grey wader of winter. The breeding dress is one of vivid brick red and can be seen occasionally in Orkney on departing birds in May or returning birds in August.

Knot (winter plumage left; summer plumage middle and right) during April at the Oyce of Quindry, South Ronaldsay – background, Kirkhouse Mill and Kirkhouse.

Purple Sandpiper • Coasts especially rocks and strandlines in autumn, winter and spring; easy to find

In Orkney flocks of up to 250 birds are not uncommon; they are present in numbers from October to early June before streaming north to breed in the short Arctic summers. Slightly plumper and bigger than Dunlin, they are restricted to rocky shores and piles of rotting seaweed where they hunt for tiny winkles and whelks. They are either very active or almost stationary. When motionless their reluctance to flush and their cryptic plumage against dark rocks and dark piles of strandline seaweed mean that their liquid restless call is often the first indication of their presence nearby. One of the tamest of waders, they can be easily overlooked. Good light highlights the understated beauty of their plumage; seeming plainly dark, shades of a muted and very subtle purple are revealed, as are their orange legs and the orange base to their bills. Ringing studies have shown that Orkney is an important wintering area and that individuals can be found feeding on the same beaches year after year. The county is equally important as a migration staging post and there are numerous instances of Purple Sandpipers stopping off in Orkney as they move between their breeding grounds and the other major wintering areas along the North Sea coasts.

Purple Sandpipers in winter on Evie pier, Evie – (l-r) Eynhallow, Eynhallow Sound and Scabra Head, Rousay

Dunlin • *Plover page, Boondie* • Coasts in autumn, winter and spring; easy to find. Moorlands in summer; hard to find

Nowadays, the most likely place to find Dunlins breeding in Orkney is high up on the hill amongst wet heather and blanket bog. Formerly they could be found in numbers on many wet lowland sites; Brodgar near the Ring for example held between 12 and 15 breeding pairs in the 1950s. Today only a handful of Dunlins nest on lowland sites and at the Ring of Brodgar there may be just a single pair. Dunlins are often found alongside or within territory held by Golden Plovers, hence the Orkney name "*Plover page*" – the two of them may even be seen standing side by side. Sometimes, their presence is given away by a neighbouring heather-nesting Skylark whose song might incorporate the Dunlin's own trilling song. Many of Orkney's breeding birds and their offspring head south in the winter – some Hoy birds have been found in Morecambe Bay, Suffolk and on Bardsey Island while a Rendall youngster was a road casualty faraway in northern Spain, fourteen months after emerging from the egg. Like a number of birds the Dunlin's summer plumage is quite different from its winter dress. This difference confounded earlier observers who regarded the summer bird and winter bird as different species. In summer plumage Dunlins exhibit a striking black belly; during the winter months this vanishes and the belly appears clean and white. At all times it has black legs and a longish slightly down-turned black bill. Around the coast in autumn, winter and spring, this is one of our commoner waders and can be found on many rocky or sandy shores and also at times on improved grassland. Many of Orkney's winter visitors arrive on our shores from Scandinavia and Russia.

Dunlins (winter plumage) in November at Ness Point, Stromness –
(l-r) Hill of Midland, Houton Head, Scapa Flow, Hoy High, Graemsay and
M.V.Hamnavoe.

Dunlin (summer plumage) in May on Muckle Bilia Fiold, Evie – background, Hill
of Huntis and Looma Shun.

Sanderlings (summer plumage left, winter plumage right) in April on Scapa
beach, St Ola – background, Scapa pier.

Sanderling • Coasts especially sand; not easy to find in autumn, winter and spring excepting Sanday

Occasionally they may be found roosting on rocks or a jetty if there is no available sand to feed on, but invariably if you want to see Sanderlings you must find the sand first. Consequently, some of the Northern Isles, especially Sanday and North Ronaldsay, both blessed with plenty of sand and importantly plenty of the right type of food, are also Sanderling-blessed with flocks of as many as 200 birds. The right type of food is a tiny worm called "*nerine*" which occurs in a narrow band of wet sand around the high water of neap tides. At other times they feed on tiny shrimp-like crustaceans that occur in the backwash of waves. It is the pursuit of these morsels which results in the "Keystone cop" antics of rushing up and down the beach as each wave breaks and recedes. Sanderlings are easily identified by their colour and habits. All identification books refer to their "clockwork toy" movements as they whirr along the shore and similar reference is made to their strikingly white winter plumage with black shoulder marks. During May and June, we have the chance to see Sanderlings in their warm salmon-pink plumage as they fatten up after arriving from South Africa during their marathon flight to Siberia – a total of 17,700 miles!

Turnstone • *Staney Putter, Stone Putter* • Coasts and occasionally short grasslands in autumn, winter and spring; very easy to find

Throughout Orkney, Turnstones are likely to be found on any shoreline during the year although they are far harder to see in June, July and August when they should be in their arctic breeding grounds. They are often in small loose flocks when feeding along the shore and in tighter groups when roosting on rocks. Occasionally they can be found feeding in improved grassland fields alongside other waders such as Lapwings or Redshanks. A rolling, chattering call just as they are taking flight or landing reveals their presence and from above the black and white chevron wing pattern is striking. At rest and in winter they appear as dumpy black and white birds; as summer approaches, increasing amounts of warm tortoiseshell pepper the plumage. At all times they have reddish-orange legs. Often it appears that the whole strandline is moving as Turnstones pick and push their way, turning stones and tangles for invertebrates. It's colloquial name in Shetland is "*Stanepecker*" or "*Ebb Pecker*", and in Norfolk, "*Tangle Picker*". The many birds that frequent the county's coastlines in winter are likely to have arrived from well within the Arctic Circle; there have been a number of instances of young birds from Ellesmere Island in northern Canada being seen along Orkney shores.

Ruff • Lowland lochs, muddy freshwater pools and grasslands in spring and autumn; very hard to find

The males in spring sport an astonishing array of ruffs and ear tufts in many colours. Unfortunately Orkney sees such examples only very rarely. Much more likely to be encountered is a tallish, upright, small-headed, lumbering and decidedly unprepossessing buff wader which visits muddy pool margins and grassland in late summer and early autumn. The best way of describing the species is "variable". The female, known as a Reeve, is much smaller than the male. This marked size variation can cause identification confusion; females maybe as small as "sandpipers" and males as big as "shanks". Leg colour is equally problematic with individuals displaying legs of all colours! In flight there can be less doubt; it appears loose winged and its tail presents two white ovals either side of a dark stripe. The largest flock in Orkney involved 127 birds in Deerness; however, most sightings are of individuals or groups of fewer than ten. In past times they were one of the most sought-after table birds and by 1850 hunting and land drainage had led to their near-extermination in Britain as a breeding bird.

Turnstones (summer plumage left, winter plumage right) in May at the Noust of Sandback, North Ronaldsay – background, the New Lighthouse.

Ruffs (and Orcas) in August at Sandside, Deerness – (l-r) Horse of Copinsay, Copinsay and Sandside Bay.

Snipe and drumming display in May at St Mary's Chapel, Wyre.

Snipe • *Horse-gowk, Water Pleep* • Wetlands, moorlands and shorelines in spring, summer and winter; very easy to find

The visual and aural aerobatic display of a Snipe is a stirring experience. High over its territory the Snipe performs an aerial circuit, a switchback ride full of sweeping climbs, glides and descents with the downward paths accompanied by a spine-tingling aboriginal cadence. Snipe breed in a variety of situations – this display can be witnessed over marshland, wet grassland and moorland. A pair of binoculars will reveal the Snipe's secret: two vibrating outer tail feathers at right angles to the tail and hitting the air on the down path. Snipe also advertise their presence by the insistent "*chip-per chip-per*" call from the ground, fence-post or dyke. Drumming in Orkney has been recorded as early as the first few days in February. During autumn time, the county is a temporary home for thousands of Snipe from the Continent – shorelines and strandlines are home to roosting birds and almost every ditch and wet hole has them busily probing with their long and fine bills, whose tips are flexible and necessarily so in order to grasp wriggling earthworms. Hard and frozen ground is difficult to probe; it is then that Snipe appear in gardens or on the roads and then that their rich patterning can best be appreciated. When disturbed, Snipe explode from the ground with a burst of sound, "*scaaap*", and tower twistingly high into the air – they are considered to be the ultimate challenge for the shotgun hunter.

Jack Snipe (and Otter) in October at the Loch of St.Tredwell's, Papa Westray – background, St. Tredwell's Chapel.

Jack Snipe • Wetlands and loch edges in autumn, winter and spring; hard to find

This is one of Orkney's most little known and secretive birds. With its smaller bill, it tends to probe less than its closest relative the Snipe, and seems to spend most of its time in dense grass and wet cover mostly near lochs. It's only when a welly-boot is hovering above does it take to the air and give the welly-wearer the fright of their life. The bird's progress is slow, low, direct, fluttering, and invariably silent with head held down before dropping back into the vegetation not too far away. There is none of the frenetic fireworks and rocket-angled flight that one normally associates with the Snipe. Consequently, the Jack Snipe is considered to be much less of a shooting challenge. However despite this it is reckoned that as many as 10,000 Jack Snipes (or *Half Snipes* as they are known in the trade) are shot in Britain each year. Birds arrive from the Continent between late September and November and during this period new, and possibly exhausted, arrivals can be located sheltering along the tideline. Most sightings or flushings are of single birds but 45 were counted during one autumn day in 1999 on North Ronaldsay. It is likely that Orkney's role is as a brief staging post for many of these Jack Snipe as they head southwest to Ireland, France and Spain.

Woodcock • Coasts, woodlands and gardens in winter and spring; hard to find

We tend to associate waders with wetland whether it is coastal or freshwater. The Woodcock does not comply – it is a bird of the woods and with its crepuscular habits, owl-like flight, 360-degree vision and stories about carrying its youngsters between its legs, is of peculiar fascination. Woodcocks choose deciduous woodland to nest in and there are records of breeding in Orkney; two nests were found on Rousay in the 19th century and since then there have been rumours of others on Hoy and Eday. It is considered to be one of the best examples of camouflage in nature; the warm and cryptic plumage blends seamlessly into the woodland floor. More normally however, we see these woodland waders in autumn. Having just crossed the North Sea from Russia and Scandinavia, fatigue means that they are likely to be seen in more unusual localities. While walking the shore or cliff line in October, a chestnut-feathered ball may explode at your feet. Neither is it uncommon to find them in the peat hill where tired birds may be brought down by Hen Harriers. As winter deepens, Woodcocks can be found in more typical situations seeking the shelter of Orkney's woodland and, occasionally, gardens in the towns and country. On one October day between 30 and 40 birds were in the fastness of Berriedale Wood on Hoy. Ringing studies have shown that some birds move on to Ireland from Orkney; a bird ringed in Holm on 14th November 2004 was shot in Donegal nine days later and a bird ringed on North Ronaldsay on 11th November 1994 was shot in Tyrone a month later. Some birds show fidelity to their wintering sites and routes in subsequent years; a bird ringed in Berstane Woods in November 1977 was recaught at the same site in December 1982.

Redshank • *Watery Pleeps* • Lowland wetlands, short grasslands, muddy freshwater pools and coasts all year; very easy to find

This is one of Orkney's most familiar birds and one of the noisiest. It's virtually impossible to walk along a stretch of shoreline or loch without being seen by a Redshank and once seen, the bird will indulge in a spot of neurotic squat thrusts before flying away and screaming its head off – hence the Orkney name "*Watery Pleeps*" and its fairly general soubriquet "*Sentinel of the Marshes*". It appears as a dusky-grey, middle-sized wader and with its red/orange legs and red/orange bill, the Redshank is one of the easiest of that tribe to identify. In flight the combination of the broad white rear-edge of the wing and the white spear-shaped rump-flash can be dazzling and is instantly recognisable. During the nesting season it can be found throughout lowland Orkney in wet habitats. Perching and bobbing on fence posts, it announces its presence in no uncertain terms and from such vantage points monitors the progress of its feeding offspring. Redshanks are rarely found in large flocks but during autumn, when visitors arrive from Iceland and Scotland, substantial loose gatherings can be found feeding on insect-rich grasslands or on coastal mud flats.

Left: Woodcock during November in Binscarth plantation, Firth – (l-r) Binscarth burn, Binscarth house and Snaba hill.

Right: Redshanks in May at the Bay of Sandside, Graemesay – (l-r) Orphir coast, Sandside and Hoy High.

93

Black-tailed Godwits (summer plumage left, winter plumage right) in late April at the Loch of Rothiesholm, Stronsay – background, Bu.

Black-tailed Godwit • Lowland wetlands, lowland lochs and muddy freshwater pools in spring, summer and autumn; hard to find

They are long-legged, long-billed and elegant. They move with grace and, in their summer chequered plumage of white, black and russet, take your breath away. In flight the black band covers half the tail and is instantly seen. Black-tailed Godwits breed in damp meadows across central and eastern Europe but for at least the last one hundred years, some of Orkney's wetlands have been blessed by their exotic presence. Birds have bred on Sanday and nowadays up to five pairs can be found in the damp meadows surrounding some of Birsay's lochs. In autumn small flocks of Icelandic birds descend on Orkney; their long fine bills probe for earthworms inland, and lugworms or ragworms at the coast. Most of them move further south and one particular Icelandic bird that was seen on its return passage on Egilsay in April 2006 is known to have spent the previous three winters at the same wintering site on the Sussex and Hampshire border. Their winter colours are less spectacular; the chestnut vanishes to be replaced by grey; however, the pied chequerboard patterns remain. In Britain, and as with Ruffs, drainage and hunting in the nineteenth century reduced their breeding numbers considerably; they were deemed to be the daintiest dish in England.

Bar-tailed Godwits (winter plumage left and right, summer plumage middle) in late April on Gritquoy Ayre, St Andrews – background, Fea Hill and the Hall of Tankerness.

Bar-tailed Godwit • *Tang Whaup* • Sand and mud flats in autumn, winter and spring; not easy to find

The two species of Godwit that occur in Orkney are very similar. In flight the tail patterns are obvious and separation is easy; however at rest, it is more difficult. The Black-tailed Godwit appears as a more elegant bird. It's slender appearance is accentuated by its long legs; the Bar-tailed's shorter legs impart an element of dumpiness. However, it is the bill shape that is telling; straight in the Black-tailed, upcurved in the Bar-tailed. Both have striking red summer plumage and both have sober grey winter plumage. Winter flocks are made up of birds that have bred in arctic Russia or Siberia and though the Bar-tailed Godwit can sometimes be found feeding in short grassland, it is more likely to be seen on soft and sandy muddy shores. Some of Orkney's favoured sites include Widewall Bay on South Ronaldsay, Scapa beach, Mill Sands in St Andrews and Sandisand in Deerness. On Sanday, Otterswick and Cata Sand have witnessed flocks composed of as many as 800 birds. The females have longer bills than the males and consequently can feed in deeper water.

Whimbrel • *May bird, Peedie Whaup* • Coasts in spring and autumn; upland in summer; not easy to find

Of the 500 pairs of Whimbrels that breed in Britain, Shetland is home to all but 25 of them. A handful of pairs are found in the Western Isles and the north Scottish mainland and the rest, about ten pairs, are found in Orkney. History tells us that pairs have been found throughout the county with recent strongholds on Eday and in the West Mainland. Despite the occasional bird remaining in Orkney over winter, most Whimbrels arrive from West Africa during late April and early May. Traditionally it has been associated with the advent of spring; hence the epithets "*May Bird*" or "*Beltane Bird*". It's at this time that their distinctive call, the seven whistles, can be heard as they fly over or are disturbed at any coastal location as they rest from the exertions of migration. Preferring an open nest site on dry heath, they breed at higher altitudes than their close relative the Curlew. Apart from their call, they differ from Curlews in having cream stripes on the head; one over each eye and the third down the crown centre. In flight their wings are darker and more uniform than the wings of the Curlew.

Whimbrels in June at Queefiglamo, Birsay – (l-r) Starra Fiold, Burn of Lushan and Starling Hill.

Right: Curlews in May at Dean, Graemsay – (l-r) Ward Hill and Cuilags, Hoy.

Along with the Lapwing, Oystercatcher and Redshank, the Curlew joins the ranks of the best known of Orkney's waders. There can be few folk who are not familiar with its profile or its voice, a voice that can be both mournful and uplifting. In springtime, the still early morning air quivers with their bubbling flight song as they float on outstretched and trembling wings to earth. They breed in a wide variety of mainly unimproved habitats including damp rushy fields, bogs and heaths, often in surprisingly high numbers. Certain areas of Orkney support Curlew colonies – as many as 55 pairs have been found in a square kilometre of lowland Rendall. Late summer sees recently cut silage fields full of Orkney Curlew families and as autumn sets in these are joined by arrivals from Scandinavia, Russia and Scotland. During the winter there may be as many as 20,000 Curlews in Orkney, amounting to 10% of the world's population; large flocks feed in short grassland or can be located roosting on the foreshore. Snowy and icy conditions mean feeding becomes harder; the longer-billed females are often forced to migrate to milder pastures well in advance of the shorter-billed males. Ringing has shown that the exodus often gravitates to the south and west; Orkney born birds have been seen during the winter in Cork, Donegal and North Uist.

Greenshanks in May on Mill Burn, Orphir
– (l-r) Waulkmill Bay, Scapa Flow, the Skaith and Veness Hill.

Greenshank • Coasts and wetlands in spring and autumn; hard to find

Nesting Redshanks are birds of wet pastures; by contrast, nesting Greenshanks are birds of wild country and choose moorland slopes, flows and pine forests. Redshanks can be found over much of Britain; Greenshanks on the other hand are restricted to the wild country of northwest Scotland and more recently a few pairs have commenced nesting in Shetland. In years past they have even bred in Orkney, with nests located in Firth and Hoy. Overall paler than Redshanks, they are also slightly larger and stand slightly taller. They differ too in their wing patterning and leg colour. Greenshanks in flight lack the Redshank's distinctive white trailing edge. In Orkney during spring and autumn, individuals are most likely to be encountered in muddy shallows and have been recorded from a wide variety of wetland sites throughout the islands. There is no one favoured locality, but the Bush, where the Loch of Stenness meets Scapa Flow, is a good bet. They catch more fish than any other wader and their feeding behaviour is characterised by forward dashes in shallow water with head and bill outstretched. Their call "te*w tew tew*" is far carrying and can be heard at night as they migrate.

Green Sandpipers in August on the Mill Dam of Rango, Sandwick – background, Kier Fiold and Kierfiold House.

Green Sandpiper • Lowland wetlands and lochs and muddy freshwater pools in spring and autumn; very hard to find

It's rare to get a good view of a Green Sandpiper. Their presence is often only noticed when they are flushed from the edge of a muddy loch. They offer only the briefest of views accompanied by their ringing *"klu-weet-weet"* call as they rise Snipe-like into the air. However in that instant you should be able to see the Green Sandpiper's salient features. It appears almost black, and the darkness of the wings and back contrasts strongly with the brilliant white of its rump, its white underbody and barred tail. As it dashes away the white rump becomes even more obvious and House Martin-like – appropriately, in Norfolk it is known as the Martin Snipe. Breeding in Russia and Scandinavia, they frequently lay their eggs in squirrel dreys or the old nests of thrushes or crows. In Orkney it is never very numerous, more are seen in autumn than spring, and the most ever recorded were nine on North Ronaldsay in September 1988. In southern England, Green Sandpipers often over-winter and favourite haunts include muddy reservoirs, sewage works, farm ponds and even garden ponds. By contrast, there has only ever been one instance of over-wintering in Orkney.

Common Sandpiper • *Steenie Pouter, Boondie, Water Pleep* • Lochs in spring and summer, coast in autumn; not easy to find

Known as the "*Summer* Snipe" by the Victorians, the Common Sandpiper arrives in April from West Africa and returns to breed on Britain's upland burns, rivers and lochs. However, unless these sites have stony shores, they are unsuitable. In Orkney, breeding Common Sandpipers are scarce but they can be found around the margins of Heldale Water and Sandy Loch on Hoy, Muckle and Peerie Water on Rousay and the Loch of Harray, the Loch of Kirbister and the lochs of the parish of Birsay in West Mainland, Often the first indication of their presence is their call, a shrill and piping "*twee-see-see*"; the next indication is of the flushed bird skimming with very shallow and rapid wing beats low over the water on strangely stiff and bowed wings. Once landed, the Common Sandpiper is at the same time curious and agitated and draws attention to itself by its conspicuous bobbing action at the water's edge. It's then that two more of its most distinctive features can be seen: the chest band and the white wedge on the side of the breast. Apart from Orkney's breeding birds, spring and autumn passage birds can occur at a wide variety of coastal and wetland sites.

Common Sandpipers in May on the Loch of Harray, Harray – background, the Merkister Hotel.

Red-necked Phalarope • *Half-web* • Lowland lochs and wetlands in spring and summer; very hard to find

This delightful role-reversing wader last bred in Orkney in 1972. Prior to that it had been known as an Orkney breeding bird from as long ago as 1800. Nesting occurred throughout Orkney including North Ronaldsay, Papa Westray, Skaill in the West Mainland and also Carness to the north of Kirkwall. However, it seems that Sanday was the stronghold with up to eight pairs in the 1920s. Red-necked Phalaropes are often associated with shallow open pools created by peat cutting. Possibly the bird's decline in Orkney reflects the long-term decline experienced by the species due to habitat loss. The role reversal mirrors that of the Dotterel – the females take the lead in courtship, copulation and fighting and have brighter plumage, while the males busy themselves with incubation duties. Unlike other waders they frequently take to swimming as they stir the loch-bottom sediments with their lobed toes in their search for food. Wintertime sees them in thousands living at sea off the southern tip of Arabia.

Red-necked Phalaropes (male left, female right) in June on the Loch of Brue, Sanday.

101

Great Skuas in May on Moor Fea, Hoy – (l-r) Rora Head, Stourdale and the Old Man of Hoy.

Great Skua • *Bonxie, Allan, Herdsman* • At sea, coasts and moorlands in spring, summer and autumn; very easy to find

There are few birds, (Magpies immediately spring to mind), that can generate such heated debate and inflamed opinions as the Great Skua. It is perceived as a heavyweight thug that will kill almost anything from birds to lambs. Indeed, no bird is safe – even some of the largest including Whooper Swans, Gannets and Grey Herons have all fallen victim. In world terms, it is not a common bird – there are more Polar Bears than Great Skuas – and the majority of the world's population is found in Shetland, Orkney, Faeroe and Iceland. Bad press has not always followed the "*Bonxie*". Once it was cherished in Shetland – known as the "*Herdsman*", it drove away the White-tailed Eagle from the lambing grounds. Later in its Shetland career, it was seen as a source of food; eggs were taken and young "*Bonxies*" were tethered and fattened-up. It is no wonder that by 1890 there were just two small colonies left in Shetland. Protection of these two colonies and a change in fishing stocks and practices led to a meteoric recovery – more food in the form of discards and an increased abundance of sand eels became available. A pair was seen on Hoy in 1908 and by the end of the century, more than 2,000 pairs were nesting throughout the county. "*Bonxie*" territories occur in the more remote areas of Orkney and are almost exclusively found on moorland. With their broad white wing flashes, guttural "*tuk-tuk-tuk*" calls and intimidating dive-bombing, the birds are easily recognisable. Ringing has demonstrated that their winter

Pomarine Skua in June harrying an Arctic Tern over Papa Sound, Stronsay – background, Papa Stronsay.

journeys range far and wide with some of Orkney's birds having been found along the western seaboard of Europe as far south as Portugal and along the southern shores of the Mediterranean Sea in Morocco, Algeria and Tunisia.

Pomarine Skua At sea and coasts in spring and autumn; very hard to find

To hardened birdwatchers who spend hours watching the sea, the sight of a Pomarine Skua with "spoons" is almost the equivalent of the Holy Grail. Breeding in the high Russian Arctic, travelling Pomarines exude an air of mystery and excitement and seeing an adult with "spoons" (the rounded and blunt ends of its long central tail feathers) simply adds to this mystery. Physically they look bulkier than an Arctic but less robust than a Great. However, identification of skuas outside spring and summer is fraught with difficulties – Arctics, Pomarines and Long-taileds can all have fairly similar plumage and both the Pomarines and the Long-taileds may have lost their tail feathers rendering them similar to Arctics. It is considered that the structure of the bird needs to be studied; compared with Arctics and Long-taileds, Pomarines are more like Bonxies – they are barrel-chested, have large heads, broad-based wings and generally give the appearance of being thickset and hefty. In Britain, summer birds can be seen in May off northwest coasts, while in autumn they rove the North Sea coasts. In Orkney look out for them from exposed coastal headlands.

Arctic Skua • *Skootie Allan* • At sea, coasts, maritime heath and moorlands in spring and summer; easy to find

You cannot but admire the aerobatic skills, the piracy and the nerve of marauding Arctic Skuas. So unlike their lumbering Great Skua cousins, robbery with violence and picking pockets has never looked so graceful. Arctic Skuas are muggers *par excellence* – auks, kittiwakes, gulls and terns are all harassed until the victim disgorges any recently caught fish. The pursuing Arctic Skua shadows and mirrors every twist and every turn of the victim's flight reminiscent of a dogfight from the First World War. Their rather derogatory local names all hinge on the misconception that it wasn't disgorged fish that they were eating but their victim's faeces. In Orkney they return to their moorland breeding colonies in late April and early May having spent the winter off the coasts of Africa; one Westray born Arctic Skua had arrived in Angola three months after hatching while a Stromness bird is known to have spent the winter in South Africa. The newly returned birds produce a "must-see" performance. The breathtaking aerial displays, involving as many as ten dashing birds, are accompanied by spine-tingling yodelling. They have been in the county longer than their Bonxie relatives; they were known in the eighteenth century with the Calf of Eday considered to be their principal breeding ground. As many as 1,000 pairs nested throughout Orkney and could be found in moorland situations on many islands. Numbers have declined by at least 50% recently probably as a result of

Arctic Skuas (light phase left, dark phase right) in June on Doomy, Eday – (l-r) Chapel Hill, Flaughton Hill and Whitemaw Hill with London airport in the foreground

the sand eel shortage. The major colonies occur on Hoy, Eday, Rousay and Papa Westray. Visually, they are very easy on the eye combining dramatic colouration and a pleasing symmetry of proportion and shape. Categorized as polymorphic, most of Orkney's Arctic Skuas are all dark birds; however, 25% of them are stunning pale-phase birds.

Long-tailed Skua • At sea and coasts in spring and autumn; very hard to find

This, the smallest of the skuas, is also the most elegant. Summer plumaged adults sport surprisingly long central tail feathers which quiver in flight. Like the Pomarine Skua it is most likely seen in May off Britain's northwest coasts and in autumn along the North Sea coasts. As with the other smaller skuas, identification becomes more difficult in autumn when the three of them exhibit similar plumages. Again, structure is the key; the Long-tailed Skua is frequently referred to as being tern-like. In Orkney look out for them in spring and autumn from exposed coastal headlands.

Long-tailed Skua (and Grey Seal) in September over Isle Rough, Copinsay – background, Copinsay farm and lighthouse.

Little Gulls (adult left, first winter right) in October on the Loch of Stenness – (l-r) the Brig o'Brodgar, the Watch Stone and the Standing Stones of Stenness with at the Brig o'Brodgar, Stenness with South Rusky Hill and the Stenness Hills in the background.

In general gulls are considered to be mean scavengers and rather too often they are simply referred to as seagulls. This is a term that encompasses every white gull from plough-following Black-headed Gulls and Common Gulls, through puffin-harrying Great Black-backed Gulls to the trawler-following Kittiwake. Superficially they appear very similar, but they all exhibit differences whether it is plumage, habitats or behaviour.

Little Gull • At sea, inshore and lochs in spring and autumn; very hard to find

Its proportions and build are tern-like as also are its feeding habits as it hawks and dips for insects over and on both sea and freshwater. It is the world's smallest gull and in Orkney, although more likely to be seen in spring and autumn, can appear at any time in the year. Normally during the winter, Little Gulls spend much of their time well offshore but the occurrence of gales occasions the arrival of birds to calmer inshore waters. They breed over a wide area of central Europe and the increased number of visits to Britain indicates that their populations are expanding – fifty years ago Little Gulls were virtually unknown to Britain. The adult plumage is stunning – black hood, pearly grey upperwings and possibly their most obvious characteristic, charcoal underwings. Young birds show a Kittiwake style "M" on their wings.

Black-headed Gulls (two adults and a juvenile) in early June on the Taing, Wyre – (l-r) Blotchnie Fiold, Knitchen Hill and Brinyan.

Black-headed Gull • *Rittock, Swarfarro* • At sea, inshore, lochs, wetlands, short grasslands, ploughed fields and towns all year; very easy to find

In their pristine spring plumage, adult Black-headed Gulls appear almost gaudy with their grey and white bodies, chocolate-brown heads and lipstick-red bills and legs. Their flash of white forewing makes them easy to identify in flight. In Britain the Black-headed Gull was for a long time a major food resource and by the end of the 19th century was considered to be close to extinction; even as late as the 1930s as many as 300,000 eggs per year were being handled at Leadenhall market. Gulls are normally associated with the sea, but Black-headed Gulls have become something of an inland gull and nationally are probably the most familiar of all; they are frequent visitors to gardens, parks and playing fields. Nowadays coastal colonies are outnumbered by those inland. In Orkney they can be found breeding on most islands usually on hill ground or grassy marshes; one of the most spectacular and easy to view colonies is that at the Mill Dam on Shapinsay. July witnesses the appearance of the unmistakeable tortoiseshell coloured young birds. As autumn approaches many of Orkney's birds move south; favoured wintering areas include the east coast of Scotland and the central belt although some individuals travel further afield and have been seen in Yorkshire and Gloucestershire. A youngster born on Sanday in June 1989 was seen on Hungerford Bridge in London in January 2003. Winter and springtime ploughing is a magnet for swirling Black-headed Gulls and the Orkney flocks are known to contain birds from Iceland and Scandinavia.

Common Gull • *White-maa, Cullya* • At sea, inshore, lochs, short grasslands, ploughed fields, wetlands and moorlands all year; very easy to find

Its name does not derive from its abundance; it comes from its choice of nesting grounds – commons or heaths. Most of Britain's Common Gulls breed in the north and west where they are found mainly on Scotland's moorland hill country, on the shore and on islands. Not uncommonly they nest with other gulls especially the Herring Gull and occasionally can be found among tern colonies. Nationally, the number of breeding birds has declined during the second half of the 20th century due to the draining of wetlands and increased afforestation. In Orkney it is the commonest of the nesting gulls and the county has up to 30% of the British breeding population. Their wild mewing calls so typical of colonies in spring can be heard from all the islands. One of the most well known colonies is that at Whaness on Hoy where unfortunately both adults and young are frequent road casualties. Orkney born birds are known to head south during autumn, some of them journeying to southern England, northern France or to the west coast of Ireland. This is also the time of year when thousands of Common Gulls from Europe are on the move. Escaping the first Continental frosts, they head for the earthworm-rich pastures and ploughed fields of Britain. Research shows that birds from Shetland, Iceland and Scandinavia make Orkney their winter home where they can be seen pursuing and harrying worm-feeding Lapwings and Golden Plovers. Common Gulls are similar to but smaller than Herring Gulls and their large brown eyes convey gentleness.

Ring-billed Gull • At sea and inshore; very hard to find

Ten years after Britain's first Ring-billed Gull was identified in South Wales in March 1973, Orkney's first was found in Stromness. A five year gap followed before Stromness was again home to this North American species and annually since then the same bird presumably has taken up a winter and spring residence in the town. There have been occasions when an adult and a youngster have been seen together raising the possibility that the youngster had accompanied one of its parents to its Orkney wintering grounds. They are hard birds to identify and easily overlooked; the odd pair could even be breeding in the county. Adult birds are similar to Common Gulls but can be separated by their bigger size, front-heavy look, yellow eyes and fierce expression. There has been a large increase in numbers in North America and this may help explain why the species is being seen increasingly in west coast towns such as Belfast, Cork, Dublin, Plymouth and Swansea.

Common Gulls nesting in May near Blubbersdale Moss, Rendall – (l-r) Cottascarth, Mid Tooin, Milldoe with Queenamidda below the mast on Fibla Fiold.

Ring-billed Gull in December at Ness Road, Stromness – background Brinkie's Brae, Stromness and Stromness harbour.

Herring Gull • *White-maa, Whitie, White-aak, Whitefool* • At sea, inshore, lochs, short grasslands, ploughed fields, wetlands and moorlands all year; very easy to find

In sharp spring sunshine when this bird is looking its finest, it's easy to understand that in Germany this seabird is known as "*Silbermowe*", that in the Netherlands it is known as "*Zilvermeeuw*" and that in Ireland it is called "*Silver Bac*" and "*Silvery Gull*". All these names are possibly far more appropriate than its English name, Herring Gull. It certainly will eat herrings but then again it will eat almost anything in its search for food. In former times it was essentially a coastal bird favouring rocky coasts, small islands and dunes but during the 20th century numbers in Europe increased meteorically principally due to its ability and versatility to exploit man-created feeding opportunities at refuse tips and sewage outfalls. With the construction of reservoirs, man also created safe daytime and nighttime roosting sites, all within easy reach of rich pickings. However, its numbers have fallen as quickly as they rose and the reasons for this decline include culling, botulism, predation from foxes and changes in the management of refuse tips which effectively now means less available food. Never high in the popularity stakes, the habit of nesting on rooftops, which was first seen on England's south coast in the 1920s, has increased its unpopularity. Even in Orkney, where there is abundance of suitable natural nesting sites, a few birds nest on roofs in Kirkwall. However, most of Orkney's birds are likely to be found on hill land where they can often be seen nesting alongside both Lesser Black-backed Gulls and Great Black-backed Gulls. On Westray, and probably elsewhere in Orkney, the young mottled-brown birds known as "*Scories*" were considered a delicacy. Herring Gulls from northern Norway and the Murmansk region descend on Orkney in November. When compared to Orkney's summer Herring Gulls, these winter visitors have considerably darker mantles, are heavily streaked about the head, have less black on their wing tips and overall appear much larger.

Lesser Black-backed Gull • *Peedie Baakie* • At sea, inshore, lochs, short grasslands, ploughed fields and moorlands in spring and summer; very easy to find

Of Orkney's three large gulls, the Lesser Black-backed Gull is the smallest and the one that spends the least time in the county. Barely one hundred years ago, Lesser Black-backed Gulls were considered true migrants spending summer in Britain and winter in North Africa. As with the other big gulls their ability to capitalise on human waste has brought about a radical change to both their numbers and their habits. The proliferation of refuse tips and the construction of nearby reservoirs has meant there is now less need for them to undertake transcontinental journeys. In 1953 just 165 Lesser Black-backed Gulls wintered in England and Wales, fifty years later there were 70,000. Unlike coastal Herring Gulls, Lessers tend to nest on the flatter areas preferring dunes and grassy slopes to rocky cliffs. They are also more inclined to nest inland where they can be found on moorland and on islands in lochs and increasingly on rooftops, including in Kirkwall. During the breeding season their bills and legs are a vivid golden yellow which added to brilliant white, brown-black and red makes for a handsome combination. Most of Orkney's colonies can be found among heather and they are frequently in the company of both Herring Gulls and Great Black-backed Gulls. By September Lesser Black-backed Gulls have left Orkney's shores; many of the adult birds head for southwest England or even Eire while the young birds may be found as far south as Portugal, Spain or Morocco. Overwintering birds are extremely uncommon and generally it is not until mid-February that the first returning birds are seen at places such as the Peedie Sea in Kirkwall or Graemeshall Loch in Holm.

Great Black-backed Gull • *Baakie, Swartback, Swarbie* • At sea, inshore, lochs, short grasslands, ploughed fields, wetlands and moorlands all year; very easy to find

Of the three large gulls that nest in Britain, the Great Black-backed Gull is the largest, most maritime and least common. With their powerful deep-chested build and upright stance they tower over both Lesser Black-backed Gulls and Herring Gulls. Adult birds seem to exude menace; they have powerful heads and a fierce expression that is emphasised by pale eyes and a steely yellow bill that seems to have been dipped in blood. They also look intensely black – their backs and wings are jet-black compared to the brown-black of the Lessers. As with the other large gulls, it takes four years for them to reach adulthood and their accompanying crisp black and white adult plumage. Younger birds show varying amounts of brown-black mottled feathering. In Britain they are birds of the north and west preferring isolated rocky cliffs, sea stacks and small islands to nest on; the largest numbers are found in Shetland, Orkney, Sutherland, the Outer Hebrides, Pembrokeshire and Scilly. They are omnivorous opportunists and from a position of near extinction in the 19th century they expanded due to a relaxation of persecution and the increased availability of fish offal at sea and refuse on land. Orkney is home to many colonies, both large and small. Some of the largest include those on Copinsay, the Calf of Eday and Rothiesholm on Stronsay. However, of late, Orkney has witnessed a drop in numbers including a very recent and marked decline

image overleaf . . .

on Hoy. Orkney youngsters travel widely in their early years and individuals have been seen in Ireland, Netherlands, France, Spain and Portugal. The adults usually become less adventurous in older age but one six-year-old Copinsay born bird was spending January in Granada in Spain. In autumn and winter, migrants from Scandinavia and Scotland arrive to supplement those Orkney birds that choose to stay.

Herring Gull (left), Lesser Black-backed Gull (middle background) and Great Black-backed Gulls (female left, male right) during June on the west side of Gallo Hill, Westray with the west Westray cliffs and the Noup in the background.

Gulls are an acquired taste but if any gull is going to inspire you, it is likely to be the Iceland Gull or the Glaucous Gull. A glimpse of either sends pulses racing and your nostrils are assailed by blasts of polar air; their wings are dipped in arctic snow and whatever their age and plumage, they resonate of the north. It appears as though part of this crystal-white iced-world has come to Orkney and icebergs, ice flows and tundra are not too distant. The first thing you notice whether the birds are on the ground or in flight is the paleness. But which species is it? Iceland Gulls and Glaucous Gulls can look very similar. In general Iceland Gulls are just about the size of a Herring Gull, have a round "Common Gull" shaped head and "gentle" appearance. Glaucous Gulls on the other hand compare very favourably in size with Great Black-backed Gulls, have heavy heads, heavy bills and look fierce and aggressive.

Iceland Gull • At sea, inshore, lochs, short grasslands and ploughed fields in autumn, winter and spring; hard to find

It appears that these arctic birds are becoming increasingly frequent in Britain and Ireland. They breed on the west and east coasts of Greenland but in the main, it is the birds from the east coast that visit Britain. There is a tendency for sightings to occur more frequently on Britain's north and west coasts; in some years the north coast of Ireland is particularly favoured as birds stream in on strong northwesterly winds from the Arctic. It may be that the decline of the fishing industry in Iceland has compelled the Iceland Gull to seek its fortune and survival further south in the winter. They are found in all those typical places where gulls congregate; preferred sites include fishing ports, refuse tips and sewage outflows. It's also not surprising to find them feeding in fields alongside other gulls, where they search for earthworms and grain. Some Iceland Gulls have been known to return to the same

"White-winged gulls" left to right: Iceland Gull first winter, Iceland Gull adult winter, Glaucous Gull first winter, Glaucous Gull adult winter during December in Hamnavoe, Stromness – background Ward Hill and the Cuilags, Hoy.

site year after year; one particular individual known as "Whitey" returned to the same site in Merseyside for 29 consecutive years. In Orkney, they can be found anywhere, but can most often be seen at the Peedie Sea in Kirkwall, Stromness harbour and Birsay Bay where they turn up annually. They are usually in ones or twos but on rare occasions as many as a dozen have been seen in Stromness and Kirkwall.

Glaucous Gull • At sea, inshore, lochs, short grasslands and ploughed fields in autumn, winter and spring; hard to find

Summer time is spent in Canada, Greenland and arctic Europe and once the breeding season is over and the northern winter begins to bite, Glaucous Gulls disperse south. Studies indicate that the Canadian and eastern Greenland birds move to North America, the western Greenland birds move to Iceland and the arctic Europe birds move into the North Sea area. As a result, often during the winter months and especially after northerly and easterly gales, Britain is on the receiving end of an influx of Glaucous Gulls. Like all other gulls, the places to look for them include fishing harbours, recently ploughed fields, rubbish tips and sewage outflows – anywhere where a free meal is on offer. Just like some Iceland Gulls, some Glaucous Gulls have a long history of returning year after year to a favoured winter haunt: two birds affectionately named "Willie" and "George" frequented the Norfolk coast each winter from 1963 to 1990. In Orkney they are never numerous; occasionally up to four may occur at one site but more usually they appear as singles. As with Iceland Gulls they can be encountered anywhere within the county, but the Peedie Sea in Kirkwall, Stromness harbour and Birsay Bay are the most frequented sites.

In order to get to grips with gulls probably one of the most foolproof, exciting and rewarding ways is to visit the Peedie Sea in winter. Either watch from a parked car by the model yacht club hut or for an experience (!) dismantle a loaf of bread from the side of the water and watch what happens. The larger gulls are generally more aloof and wary; it is the Common Gulls and Black-headed Gulls that make the first appearance. The Great Black-backed Gulls rarely deign to pick up a crumb.

Gulls in winter – from smallest to biggest

Black-headed Gull – the smallest of the gulls on show with both adults and younger birds present. Most of the adults will still be in winter plumage and black heads will not usually be visible. The features to look for on the adults are their pale grey mantles, the small black spot behind the eye, red legs, red bills and a startling white forewing in flight. Young birds will appear more mottled with brown markings in their wings, have a dark spot behind the eye and a black band at the end of their tail. Their feet and bills are dull yellow.

Common Gull – next in size and slightly bigger and more robust than the Black-headed Gull but a lot smaller than the similarly coloured Herring Gulls. The adults are white with a distinct blue-

Winter plumaged gulls during March at the Peedie Sea, Kirkwall with the Staatsrat Lehmkuhl in the background.

grey mantle, their heads are flecked with dusky markings, and they have yellow bills and yellow legs. One of the most obvious features is their "soft" dark eye. Young birds are mottled with brown markings in their wings, dusky flecks on their heads and a black tail band. They have pink legs and pink bill with a black tip.

Herring Gull – much bigger than both Black-headed Gulls and Common Gulls. The adults are pale grey and white, have dusky streaked heads, pink legs and a bright yellow bill with a red spot at the tip. Young Herring Gulls appear in various stages of plumage. The youngest birds are mottled brown with older birds showing slightly greyer on their mantle and in their wings with each successive year until they reach adult plumage after four years. They have dark bills and legs. 'Northern' Herring Gulls arrive in November. They look bigger, have heavily streaked heads, darker mantles and less black on their wing tips.

Great Black-backed Gull – the largest and wariest species present. The adults are jet black and white with dusky streaks on the head, pink legs and yellow bills with a red spot. Young birds take four years to attain adult plumage. The youngest are mottled pale brown and appear much paler than young Herring Gulls. Older birds exhibit increasing amounts of black on their mantles and in their wings. They have dark bills and pink legs.

Standing birds left to right: Black-headed Gull adult winter; Common Gull adult winter; Herring Gull adult winter; Great Black-backed Gull adult winter .

Flying birds left to right: Black-headed Gull first winter; Common Gull first winter; Herring Gull first winter; Great Black-backed Gull first winter.

Sandwich Terns (and Common Seals) in April at South Wick, Papa Westray-background, Holm of Papa Westray.

Sandwich Tern • At sea, inshore and coasts in spring, summer and autumn; easy to find

After the dark days of winter, there are few more welcoming sounds than the creaky cry of the Sandwich Tern fresh back from a winter off the West African coasts. Along with Wheatears, Sand Martins and Chiffchaffs, they represent the first wave of returning African migrants and by late March, looking brilliant white against any colour of sea, they are fishing in sheltered Orkney waters and renting the air with their distinctly un-oiled calls. Sandwich Terns are essentially coastal and nest on sand, shingle and occasionally turf-covered islets. Many of their nesting sites are traditional and they can often be found in association with Black-headed Gulls whose presence provides a strong element of protection. Colonies in Britain are widely scattered and Orkney's only colony, which is found on Papa Westray, represents the most northerly in the UK. As well as being the earliest of the terns to arrive, it is also the latest to leave; November birds are frequently seen and quite surprisingly, there have been instances of small numbers spending the winter in Orkney. Most however head off to spend winter along the length of the West African coast as far south as Cape Province in South Africa. There have also been instances of Orkney born birds leaving the county to nest in Denmark and the Netherlands. With its raucous cry, yellow-tipped black bill and its overall shaggy-headed appearance, it is one of the easier terns to identify.

Little Tern • At sea, inshore and coasts in spring, summer and autumn; very hard to find

This, the smallest of Britain's terns, leads a life fraught with difficulties. Often nesting so close to the high tide line that flooding is a distinct possibility, its survival is further compounded by choosing beaches where recreational pressure is at its greatest. Consequently they flourish best where access is limited. In Britain there are less than 3,000 pairs, with most of them nesting in eastern England where beach pressure is not inconsiderable. In Orkney, they are annual visitors in very low numbers and since the end of the 20th century a handful of pairs have nested at suitable sandy sites on North Ronaldsay, Sanday, Egilsay, Burray and South Ronaldsay. Tiny, dainty, very noisy and with an orange bill and white forehead they are, once found, very conspicuous and pay the observer as much attention, and sometimes more, as the observer pays to them.

Arctic Tern • *Pickie-terno, Ritto, Rittock, Tirrick* • At sea, inshore and coasts in spring, summer and autumn; very easy to find

The vast majority of Britain's Arctic Terns nest in Scotland and while the Common Tern frequently nests inland, the Arctic Tern is almost exclusively coastal. It leads a life of wandering and in the course of a calendar year can circumnavigate the planet. Colonies have been located in Greenland just 700km from the North Pole, and wintering birds have been observed in Antarctica. At some time or other over the course of the winter, Orkney's birds fly the length of the West African coast; the speed of travel is almost unbelievable and is defined by a young bird from Westray that was ringed on 5th July 2002 and found in Cape Province, South Africa on 5th October, just twelve weeks later. Possibly because of the huge journeys it undertakes, the Arctic Tern spends less time in Orkney than the other terns. Having arrived to breed during May, by August most birds, adults and offspring alike, have left the county. In Orkney it has always been considered as an abundant summer visitor breeding on shingle, sand, turf-covered rock stacks, grassland and even on the hill. There can be over 200 colonies within Orkney, ranging from a handful of pairs up to thousands. In recent years, Orkney was home to almost 40% of the European breeding population with large colonies on Papa Westray, Auskerry, Flotta, Swona, Pentland Skerries, Hoy and Rousay. On Papa Westray alone, 17,000 pairs were counted in 1969. Arctic Terns have fared poorly of late; a shortage of sand eels has led to a succession of poor breeding seasons and there have been instances in recent years of complete failure.

Common Tern • *Pickie-terno, Ritto, Rittock* • At sea, inshore and coasts in spring, summer and autumn; not easy to find

There are great similarities between Common Terns and Arctic Terns. Older textbooks relied on museum specimens to highlight differences between the species but many of these characteristics could not be seen adequately in the field. Confident separation has only been possible since the advent of better optical equipment and new identification studies. It's probable that differentiation of the two species in Orkney is a fairly recent event, possibly confirmed by the fact that both species have been given the same Orkney names. Compared with Arctic Terns, Common Terns are bulkier, have an orange bill with a black tip and usually show a black wedge-shaped mark on the upper side of the wing towards the tip – the last feature can be seen from a kilometre away. In Britain, the Common Tern is more widely distributed than the Arctic and can often be found at inland sites such as gravel pits where artificial nest sites in the form of rafts have proved exceptionally popular. In Orkney there may be no more than 200 nesting birds, the majority on the wooden pier at Lyness, Hoy or on islands in the Loch of Stenness.

Left: Arctic Terns in May at Ossin, Egilsay – background, Howan.

Common Terns in May at Little Vasa Water, Shapinsay – background, the Bay of Furrowend and Furrowend.

Kittiwake • *Kittick, Kittiwaako* • At sea, inshore and cliffs in spring, summer and autumn; very easy to find

With their wild cries ringing as they wheel and turn in the updraughts, Kittiwakes bring energy and grace to Britain's cliff-nesting seabird colonies. Rarely do they look anything other than clean-cut and smart; their simple plumage of grey, white and black sounds prosaic but is crisp and striking. Except in the winter, when greys smudge the head, there are no blurred edges; the wing tips truly appear as though they were "dipped in black ink", as do their feet and legs. Even their immature plumage is smart, a black boa on their nape and a jet black "M" on their wings, described with the skill of a calligrapher. In fact their feathers were much sought-after; in the 19th century, the millinery trade was responsible for the extermination of whole colonies. They were also shot for sport and for food, their flesh being described "as good as partridge". In the main, they breed on the most sheer, precipitous and featureless of cliffs and the locations of some of their nests appear to defy the laws of gravity. They are the most maritime of Britain's breeding gulls and are seldom seen inland. During winter flocks are often seen hundreds of miles from land; many of Orkney's young Kittiwakes range over the North Sea and travel to the Mediterranean but some fly as far afield as Greenland or Labrador and Newfoundland in Canada. As sprats and herring move north in spring, the Kittiwakes return to their cliff sites. Nest building is a major priority and the spectacular to-ing and fro-ing of Kittiwakes with beakfuls of muddy vegetation can be observed at localities such as Mar Wick Bay and Mull Head LNR in Deerness. Orkney is very important for Kittiwakes; there may be as many as 60,000 pairs here, which equates to about 20% of Britain's population. However, in recent years, a marked shortage of sand eels has led to difficult times for young Kittiwakes and there has been a sequence of poor breeding seasons for adults.

Guillemot • *Aak, Skout, Lungi* • At sea, inshore and cliffs in spring, summer and autumn; very easy to find

Scotland has 80% of the Guillemots that breed in Britain; there are 28 colonies with more than 10,000 birds. What makes Scotland so special is its proximity to vast quantities of marine food that occur where the warm waters of the North Atlantic Drift meet the cooler waters of northern Europe. Geology also lends itself to convenient nesting – Scotland's cliff ledges, most of them inaccessible to ground predators, are second to none. Some of Scotland's largest colonies, known as loomeries occur in Orkney where there are estimated to be 180,000 birds; the cliffs of west Westray hold 70,000 birds and both Marwick Head and Copinsay support 30,000 birds. Look carefully and among them will be the variety known as "bridled" Guillemots, the further north you go the more common they become. In Orkney one out of every seven is "bridled" while in Shetland it becomes one out of four. With such overall abundance, it's no surprise to learn that Guillemots' flesh, eggs and feathers were exploited in Orkney for centuries – "swappin for aaks" was last noted on Papa Westray in the 1920s. Packed like rows of milk bottles on doorsteps, Guillemots, with just two square inches, have the smallest nesting territory of any bird. They are noisy birds; their loud murrings giving rise to their North American name "*murre*". They have a single, pear-shaped and uniquely marked colourful egg whose shape, in theory, means that it is less likely to roll off a narrow and packed ledge. With short, stubby wings and streamlined shape they excel underwater; their foraging can take them to depths of up to 200 metres. At the end of the breeding season and with winter approaching Orkney's cliffs are vacated and Guillemots travel into the North Sea, the English Channel and the Bay of Biscay. Conversely, ringing has also demonstrated that Guillemots born on both the west and east coasts of Scotland journey to Orkney waters to spend winter. One of these birds was a youngster ringed on the Isle of Canna in June 1974 – thirty years later it was found freshly dead in November 2004 on the shores of Veantrow Bay on Shapinsay.

Razorbill • *Coulter-neb, Baukie* • At sea, inshore and cliffs in spring, summer and autumn; very easy to find

As important as Scotland is for Guillemots, it is probably even more important for their close cousin the Razorbill; two out of every five Razorbills in Europe nest in Scotland. In appearance they are quite similar but take note of the Razorbill's much blacker plumage and its heavy, broad chisel bill etched with white lines. Additionally Razorbills are less dependent on sheer cliffs and tend to avoid the crowded Guillemot ledges; their preference is to be discreet, consequently cavities in cliff faces, and even rabbit burrows, are chosen where a single large egg is incubated. Quite extraordinarily this egg weighs a seventh of the mother's bodyweight. In Orkney, Razorbills are far less numerous than Guillemots, but can be found nesting wherever there are high and rocky cliffs. Of the county's 10,000 breeding birds up to 4,000 can be found in west Westray with other substantial gatherings at Marwick Head and Copinsay. At three weeks old, youngsters descend to the sea at night to avoid predators such as Great Black-backed Gulls; the single chick is cared for by the father for a further two or three months. Like many of Orkney's auks, "*le petit pingouin*", as it is known in France, heads for the coastal waters of the North Sea, English Channel and the Bay of Biscay for the months of winter. Ringing has indicated that those Razorbills that appear in Orkney during the winter may originate from Iceland, Norway or western Scotland.

image overleaf . . .

*Kittiwakes, Guillemots and Razorbills in June on Lobust, Rousay –
background, Sacquoy Head*

Kittiwakes – two adults and two juveniles on cliffs; one adult and one juvenile flying; one in winter plumage on pier stake.

Guillemots – twelve adults on cliffs including one 'bridled' Guillemot; one in winter plumage on sea at bottom right.

Razorbills – two adults on cliffs; one adult in winter plumage on sea at bottom right.

Black Guillemots (three in summer plumage; right hand bird in winter plumage) in April on Papa Sound, Stronsay – background, Whitehall village and old pier.

Black Guillemot
- *Tystie, Tyste*

- At sea, inshore and cliffs all year; very easy to find

There can be few birds whose plumage changes so completely within twelve months. In the summer, the Black Guillemot is strikingly visible; a black bird with brilliant white oval wing patches. In the winter, it is a grey and white bird, still sporting the white oval wing patches, but nearly invisible in a wintry sea. Equally bizarre is its call; it's difficult to imagine this thin piping whistle being produced by a seabird but it is this strange call, the "*peisti*" of Old Norse, which gives the Black Guillemot its northern name "*Tystie*". In Britain, the "*Tystie's*" strongholds are Ireland and the west coast of Scotland. Generally nesting on rocky and boulder strewn coasts, it occasionally chooses rabbit holes and artificial nest sites such as old buildings, holes in wooden piers and even the barrels of cannons. Butterfish are a favourite "*Tystie*" food. In Orkney, Black Guillemots can be seen at all times of the year but are particularly impressive during the early part of the breeding season when small groups engage in communal displays that include underwater swimming chases and water dancing. In the evening, roosting birds congregate on buoys or fish farm rafts. Scapa Flow is nationally important for "*Tysties*" and can hold almost 1,000 birds – this represents nearly 3% of the British wintering total. Throughout their British range Black Guillemots are sedentary birds; Orkney youngsters had been found no further afield than the Dornoch Firth until one was located off the Dutch coast five years after being ringed on Swona.

*Puffins nesting in June
on the Castle o'Burrian, Westray.*

Puffin • *Tammy-norrie, Lyer, Lyre, Bottlenose, Pope, Sea Coulter* • At sea, inshore and cliffs all year; not easy to find

There's no British bird quite like the Puffin – seeing one is guaranteed to put a smile on a face and uplift the lowest of spirits. Apart from their colourful and patterned clown-faces that present an expression of sadness, doom and depression, they usually allow the observer a confiding intimacy that most other birds do not. Winter is usually spent at sea; Orkney birds have been located off the Portuguese, Spanish, Italian and North African coasts and even as far afield as Newfoundland. During this time their plumage turns duskier and their bills lose much of their colour. Puffins return to Orkney waters in March in preparation for their summer residency that lasts till early August. They are primarily burrowers but can also be found tenanting holes and crevices in cliff faces. They have more of a tendency to nest on offshore islands than Guillemots and Razorbills and in Orkney the largest colony is on remote Sule Skerry where there are 60,000 occupied burrows. Auskerry, Copinsay, the Pentland Skerries, Switha and Swona are all Puffin strongholds as are the cliffs of Hoy and Westray. Research has illustrated that it is not uncommon for Puffins born at other colonies such as the Farne Islands and the Isle of May to come to Orkney to breed. Fish, small squid and planktonic crustaceans are their principal diet. One dexterous Puffin was observed with 61 sand eels in its bill, all at the same time, but as with other seabirds, the recent shortage of sand eels in northern waters has affected their welfare.

Little Auk • *Rotchie* • At sea and inshore in winter; hard to find

This tiny seabird, no bigger than a Starling, breeds beyond the Arctic Circle in some of the world's most snowbound and inaccessible localities. With a population of approximately 30 million, it is considered to be the world's most numerous seabird. However, its pelagic habits and its remote breeding sites mean that in normal circumstances it is one of the most difficult of birds to see. Little Auks, unlike the other British auks, feed almost exclusively on planktonic crustaceans and autumn storms in the northern seas may mean that food becomes hard to find. Subsequently hordes of Little Auks disperse from the northern fastness to seek winter sustenance and it is at this time that we may be privileged to see these waifs. In Orkney, birds are seen in most years between October and March and may turn up anywhere. Sometimes flights of them are recorded passing into the North Sea, at other times storm-driven birds are located sheltering inshore and on occasion birds are even found well inland. Apparently over the winter of 1894/5 there were thousands in Kirkwall Bay. One favoured location seems to be the southeastern sector of Scapa Flow in the shadow of the Holm cliffs and the Churchill Barriers.

Great Auk • At sea, inshore and cliffs all year; impossible to find

The extinction of the Great Auk makes for sad reading. Its flightless condition and tameness encouraged the belief that it was "God's admirable instrument for the sustentation of man". At some time in its history this bird, which stood 75cm tall, was found throughout the coasts of the north Atlantic including North America, Greenland, Iceland and Europe. However, by the middle of the nineteenth century the penguin of the northern hemisphere was no more. The death and fate of Orkney's last two birds is well

Little Auks in December in the Bay of Legrow, St Mary's village, Holm – background, 17ᵗʰcentury storehouse and No1 barrier.

Right: Great Auk in April 1813 on Fowl Craig, Papa Westray – background, looming extinction.

documented. At Fowl Craig on Papa Westray, the female was stoned to death on her nest in 1812 and the male the following year. The female became Lot 43 "A very fine specimen of this exceedingly rare bird...the only one taken on the British coast for many years, and an egg, in a glass case, £16:5:6d". A cairn and monument erected by the junior members of the Orkney Field Club commemorates the Papay birds. Great Auk bones have been located at archaeological sites in Holm, Birsay and Rousay.

Rock Doves in October feeding in a 'neep' field at Bow, Flotta – (l-r) Switha and Cantick Head lighthouse, South Walls.

Rock Dove • *Doo* • Cliffs, cereal stubbles, set-aside all year; very easy to find

Throughout most of Britain, it is difficult to separate the Rock Dove from the Feral Pigeon. True Rock Doves are essentially birds of coastal cliffs where they nest colonially in sea caves, on ledges or even among boulders. The purest colonies in Britain occur on remote northern and western sea cliffs well away from the semi-domesticated dovecote and racing pigeon communities that have infiltrated the wild populations elsewhere. Authentic Rock Doves can be recognised by their consistent plumage characteristics that include two black wing bars, unspotted wing coverts and a white lower back, rump and underwing. Geographically, Orkney can be regarded as a pure colony, but even here one or two "moles" can always be uncovered when a roost of Rock Doves is disturbed from the cliffs. It is hardly surprising given that for at least 700 years, dovecotes were both an integral part of Orkney's rural economy and a major source of protein. They are prolific breeders and it is not unknown for pairs to raise five or six broods per year. During wintertime flocks of up to 1,000 birds can be found feeding in cereal stubbles or set-aside.

Woodpigeons in April in Willow Woods, Kirkwall
– background, Willow Burn, Willow Road and St Magnus Cathedral.

Woodpigeon • Woodlands, gardens, cereal stubbles, set-aside all year; easy to find

The development of new agricultural crops over the last 200 years transformed the Woodpigeon from a bird of deciduous forests, relying solely on natural foods such as beechmast, acorns and ivy berries, to a bird of farmland. More especially it was the widespread practice of growing turnips for winter fodder and undersowing corn with clover that helped it consolidate its range. By the turn of the 20th century they were breeding in the Outer Hebrides and Orkney and are now resident in Shetland and Faeroe. From 1840, the year of its first appearance in Orkney, the Woodpigeon increased swiftly, initially nesting in the woodlands of Binscarth, Balfour, Berstane, Melsetter and Muddisdale. It is an adaptable bird and where trees are unavailable for nesting, it will nest in heather. By the end of the 20th century almost all of the county's inhabited islands were occupied. Ringing has shown that Orkney birds frequently move between the islands for feeding and nesting purposes and one individual, ringed as a chick in May 1981 at Berstane Woods reached the grand age of 18 before being found dead at Crantit in February 1999. Bigger than Rock Doves, Woodpigeons are recognised by their wine coloured breast, white collar and white wingbars, the last being especially evident during the graceful soaring display flights which are accompanied by wing clapping.

Collared Dove • Gardens and woodlands all year; very easy to find

In 1930, the nearest Collared Doves to Britain were in the Balkans. By 1943 they had spread to Germany, by 1950 to France and by 1955 to England. On 23rd July 1962, Orkney's first Collared Dove was recorded in St Margaret's Hope and in the following year not only were there sightings from Kirkwall, Binscarth and Rousay but also a partly built nest was found in Balfour Castle Woods on Shapinsay. A nest with seven eggs was found in Binscarth in 1964 and since then Collared Doves have continued to expand their range in the county. The birds are closely associated with human habitation principally where grain is available and nowadays they can be found throughout all the inhabited islands. The expansion has slowed down considerably but pairs are still colonising new locations particularly in the country. Sizeable populations can be found in Kirkwall, Stromness, St Margaret's Hope and Finstown especially where garden bird feeders are in good supply. Finstown, seemingly with feeders in every garden, is notably favoured and in winter can attract flocks of 100 birds. An example of surprising longevity is provided by one of the earlier birds that was ringed as an adult on Fair Isle in June 1975 and found dead in St Margaret's Hope 24 years later in February 1999. Collared Doves are prolific breeders and are capable of having numerous clutches during a breeding season that may last for more than six months. Dressed in soft buff and with a clerical black half collar they are dainty, long-tailed doves, whose persistent cooing does not find favour with everyone.

Turtle Dove • Coast, woodlands and gardens in spring and autumn; very hard to find

It's sobering information that three quarters of its population has been lost in the last thirty years. The Turtle Dove is Europe's only migratory dove and like many other Africa to Europe migrants must contend with Mediterranean gun slinging. In Malta alone 100,000 Turtle Doves are shot annually. This, coupled with the increased use of herbicides resulting in shortages of food and the desertification of its winter pastures, paints a bleak picture. In Britain it is typically associated with the light and dry arable farmland found in the southeast and like the Woodpigeon increased its range as new methods of arable cultivation developed in the 19th century. During this period it could be found in southeast Scotland but its present troubles have ensured a range contraction and its distinctive purring song is less widely heard. A few migrant individuals appear in Orkney each year, primarily in May and October. It is smaller than the Collared Dove and has red-brown upperparts.

Left: Collared Doves in summer at Fribo House, Westray.

Turtle Dove in May at Holland, North Ronaldsay.

Left: Great Spotted Woodpecker in November at St Magnus Cathedral, Kirkwall.

Right: Long-eared Owl in November roosting at Smiddybanks, Pier Road, St.Margaret's Hope, South Ronaldsay – background, the Hope.

Great Spotted Woodpecker • Woodlands and gardens in winter; very hard to find

Some birds irrupt – this is one of them! Others that fall under this label are the Waxwing and the Crossbill. The cause of the irruption is usually a lack of food in their breeding grounds so hungry birds urgently have to find another source of food. The Great Spotted Woodpeckers that irrupt into Orkney probably have crossed the North Sea from Scandinavia or central Europe. In those areas, it may be that there has been a poor seed crop especially of pine and spruce, and easterly winds have brought them to these islands. But will they find what they want here? Probably not! In some years there are no sightings in Orkney, but other years can provide a great bounty. Look out for them in wooded areas such as St Magnus cathedral, Willow Road or Papdale in Kirkwall or Binscarth in Finstown. Most sightings occur in the autumn and early winter but in 1976 a bird was heard drumming in June and July at Trumland, Rousay. Except for the far north of Scotland, Great Spotted Woodpeckers can be found breeding in deciduous woodland throughout Britain.

Long-eared Owl

● Woodlands in autumn,
winter and spring; hard to find

Plumage-wise, the Long-eared Owl is very similar to its close relative the Short-eared Owl. However, if you are fortunate enough to see a Long-eared Owl during the day, it gives the impression of being a much darker-coloured bird. This is a typical owl in that, invariably, it only comes out at night. Unlike the Short-eared Owl though, this owl needs trees to nest in and though not nesting every year in Orkney, there have been several instances of breeding at suitable sites such as Melsetter on Hoy, Binscarth in Firth and Carrick on Eday. With the increase in tree planting within the county, it may be that nesting becomes more frequent and widespread and the far-carrying nocturnal hooting may be heard more commonly. During October, Long-eared Owls arrive in Orkney from Europe, some from as far afield as Russia and frequent traditional roost sites during the day. Ringing has illustrated that the same birds often return to the same Orkney sites year after year. Perched motionless and silent, and cryptically plumaged, Long-eared Owls can be found in any shelter, from a luxuriant patch of conifers to a scrubby fuchsia hedge. The dissection of pellets that accumulate at traditional roost sites indicates that the Orkney Vole is the principal prey item. In Britain, breeding birds can be found in a wide variety of woodland situations especially where nearby open ground supports an abundance of mammal prey.

Cuckoo • *Gauk* • Moorlands near scrub and woodlands in spring, summer and autumn; very hard to find

Although the Cuckoo has never been a common bird in Orkney, each year there are widespread reports of its presence. Some of these reports will relate to birds that have found Orkney by mistake due to adverse winds, but there are also hearings and sightings of birds that are intent on staying within the county to breed. It is a late arriver, often not seen or heard until mid May and it is quite catholic in its choice of habitats and also in its choice of birds to parasitise. In Britain where it breeds widely and in many different habitats, the most common host birds are Dunnocks, Meadow Pipits and Reed Warblers. Reed Warblers do not occur as breeding birds in Orkney, and with only a handful of breeding Dunnocks, it is likely that Meadow Pipits will be the preferred option. However, in 1975, adult Skylarks were observed raising a Cuckoo chick. Look out for Cuckoos from mid May until the end of June. In flight, they bear more than a passing resemblance to Sparrowhawks so be aware of small birds mobbing what appears to be a raptor – it could be a Cuckoo. Their trademark call may be uttered from on high in or near areas of Orkney woodland.

Cuckoo in June at Roeberry, South Ronaldsay – background, Uppertown and Sands of Wright.

136

Short-eared Owl • *Cattie-face, Cattie-ogle* • Moorlands and rough grasslands all year; easy to find

The sight of a honey-coloured Short-eared Owl hunting over rough fields or perched atop a roadside post is always guaranteed to uplift the grimmest of moods. Most owls are abroad at night, but the "*Cattie-face*" can be seen during daylight throughout the county and for most of the year. It is during winter when they become a little bit harder to see; the longer winter nights mean that they become more nocturnal. Additionally, research has shown that some birds leave Orkney altogether – most probably they head for the mainland of Scotland but a chick that was ringed in Firth during May 1983 was shot in the following October in the Basque region of Spain. Nests are made in heather and rushes during May and often the parents raise two or even three youngsters. Owl activity is at its greatest in June and July when the young are at their most demanding. Both parents are seemingly pressed into continuous action hunting for Orkney voles, rats and rabbits to supply the ever-open mouths. It is even possible to distinguish between the mother and the father; the female is usually much darker than the male. Recent estimates indicate that Orkney may support up to 70 pairs. Breeding occurs on Eday, Hoy, Mainland, Rousay, Sanday, South Ronaldsay and Stronsay. Most of Britain's Short-eared Owls nest on heather moorland especially in the north of England and Scotland; however, a few nest in young forestry plantations and in coastal rough grazing.

Short-eared Owls in June at Kirkwall airport, Grimsetter, St Andrews.

137

Swifts in July over Finstown, Firth – (l-r) the Kame of Hoy and the Lochs of Harray and Stenness in the background; the A965, Binscarth, the Ouse and the Bay of Firth in the foreground.

Swift • Overhead and feeding over lochs in mid summer; hard to find

Just about all of its non-breeding life is spent scything through the air on its distinctive scimitar-shaped wings and it can justifiably be described as Britain's most aerial bird. It is totally dependent on a rich supply of airborne insects and spiders; consequently as a breeding bird it is commonest in the drier and warmer parts of Britain and scarcer in the cooler and wetter north and west. It is one of our shortest staying summer visitors and is rarely with us for longer than three months; it arrives late (usually May) and leaves early (usually August). Although known to nest in crevices in sea cliffs or even holes in trees, the great majority of Swifts utilise the eaves of older buildings in areas of long-established occupation. Periods of cold, wet and windy weather mean that food finding is difficult; the adult birds may be forced to fly huge distances around weather depressions in their search for suitable food. Swift chicks are able to withstand these food shortages by going into a state of torpor for up to forty-eight hours. Considered throughout much of the United Kingdom as an emblem of summer, this description is inappropriate for cool Orkney. As yet it has not bred in the county and sightings, usually involving small numbers of birds, are infrequent between June and August.

House Martins in July hawking for insects near Noltland Castle, Westray

House Martin

• Modern houses and feeding over lochs; not easy to find

We still have little idea as to where House Martins go during the British winter. They are distinctly aerial and possibly they spend most of their time on the wing, even sleeping, high above African forests. Their return to Britain is later than that of Sand Martins and Swallows; often it's May before we see them in Orkney and its distinctive buzzy call, white rump and blue-black plumage is a welcome sight of summer as it hawks for insects over lochs or reedbeds. Sea cliffs have been used for nest sites but generally they have a close affinity with man; large colonies are often associated with farmyards, bridges and long-established buildings and in Orkney, House Martins built in the corners of the windows of St Magnus Cathedral during the 19th century. In more recent times they appear to have developed an attachment to the eaves of modern houses and it is at such sites, most faithfully in Holm, Finstown, Stromness and Birsay where the majority of Orkney's breeding birds can be found constructing their conspicuous mud nests. With the provision of artificial nest boxes in the important House Martin areas in the county, it is reckoned that the population has increased to just over 30 pairs. In recent years adventurous pairs have raised young in Pierowall on Westray and at the Sanday School. Orkney is at the northern edge of its range, but some more adventurous birds have even nested successfully north of the Arctic Circle.

Swallow • Farms, WW2 buildings and over lochs; very easy to find

During the 19th century, a small number of Swallows bred in Kirkwall chimneys and on St Magnus Cathedral. A dramatic increase of late means that their chattering calls and swooping, gliding flight are familiar in summer throughout Orkney. The 50 pairs of 1982 are now closer to 500 pairs. Swallows like farms with traditional buildings and livestock and Orkney is blessed with plenty of both; buildings provide safe nesting locations and grazing livestock stirs up large numbers of flies to feed on. Other typical sites include piers, bridges and derelict World War 2 emplacements. After winter in South Africa, it's usually mid April by the time they return to Orkney and are seen either at their previous year's nest sites, prospecting new sites or hawking over lochs. The mud and saliva nests are lined with fine hairs and feathers, and with maintenance, can last years (one is on record as being used for almost 50 years). Two or rarely three broods may be raised; by August, family parties congregate on overhead lines and fences ready for the marathon and perilous journey to Africa. As many as 2,000 birds may roost in the Graemeshall Loch reed bed prior to departure. An indication of the speed with which they can migrate is exemplified by an Orkney chick that was initially ringed on 6th August 2003, subsequently recaught at the Loch of Graemeshall roost on 8th September and once more caught on 12th October in Zaragoza, northern Spain. In Britain, except for upland areas, they can be found nesting almost everywhere; however, there have been declines in east and south England due to changes in farming practices including the use of pesticides and the construction of modern Swallow unfriendly buildings.

Sand Martin • *Witchuck* • Feeding over lochs in spring, summer and autumn; hard to find

This, the most water-loving of the family known as hirundines, was once a lot more frequent as a breeding bird in Orkney than it is now. In the eighteenth century this small, brown and white swallow, with its distinct breast band, was considered the commonest of the clan and bred in the banks of the Stenness and Skaill lochs and on Sanday. When hand cutting of peat was more widespread, it may even have bred in drying peat stacks as it does in Ireland, There have been fewer breeding records in recent years although in the first years of the 21st century a handful of pairs has bred annually in suitable vertical sand faces. In Britain, its distribution is constrained by geology. Sand Martin burrows are found almost exclusively in sand; natural sites include riverbanks and manmade sites include railway cuttings, road cuttings and sand and gravel pits. An opportunistic nester, colonies can be hundreds strong and it has benefited from the post-war boom in road and house building and the consequent opening up of new sand quarries. After a winter in the Sahel region of Africa, birds return to Britain in late March; in Orkney they are most likely to be encountered hawking for insects over lochs during April and May.

Left: Swallows in May at Scar, Sanday – background, Scar and Smithcot.

Sand Martins in June at Scapa, St Ola – (l-r) Scapa beach, Scapa distillery, OIC harbours department, Royal Oak interpretation centre and Wideford Hill.

141

Skylark • *Laverock, Lavero, Lady's Hen*

• Uplands, grasslands, cereal stubbles,
set-aside all year; very easy to find

It's almost impossible to imagine how abundant Skylarks were in Britain in previous centuries. Widely exploited as a food, Skylarks in the 16th century were the birds that "chiefly garnished men's tables in winter" and, in the late 19th century, Leadenhall market in London took in approximately 400,000 birds per annum with up to 40,000 a day in some cases; the chief killing fields were the downlands of Sussex, Cambridgeshire and Bedfordshire. A pie of 300 Skylarks was part of the opening of the Forth Railway Bridge celebratory dinner. It's difficult to believe that this relentless harvest has not affected Skylark fortunes but in actual fact they remain one of the most widely distributed birds of Britain and Ireland and their song is a constant accompaniment to a springtime visit to open country from the coast to high upland. However, their numbers have declined; agricultural changes over the last thirty years have brought about a shortage of winter food and springtime breeding habitat. Even in Orkney, a decline has been observed but they can still be found in cultivated and grassland habitats – the RSPB reserve on Egilsay has at least 100 territories. Many birds leave Orkney for the winter, those that remain can usually be found in cereal stubbles or set-aside. They are plump, pot-bellied, heavy-billed and big-eyed. Their plumage is not striking, a mixture of grey, brown and buff streaks, and in flight a white trailing edge to the wing. But they have their heavenly song – described by poets as a silver chain of sound. Mostly it is delivered from on high but occasionally they can be seen singing from fence posts.

Left: Skylarks in April at the cenotaph to the Martyrdom of St Magnus, Egilsay – (l-r) Manse Loch, Muckle Green Holm, Howan and Shapinsay.

Meadow Pipit in April at Graemeshall, Rendall with Gairsay in the background.

Meadow Pipit • *Teeting, Titlark* • Uplands and grasslands all year; very easy to find

This slender and fine-featured bird is a blend of browns, olives and buffs. It has streaks and flesh-coloured legs. Uttering a plaintive and thin "*tseep tseep tseep*" while flying, it is then that the white outer tail feathers can be glimpsed. Like the Skylark, the Meadow Pipit, is a bird of open country and has an uplifting spring song and parachute display guaranteed to dispel any lingering winter darkness. It appears delicate and fragile, but is genuinely hardy and can be found in Britain from sea level to 1,000 metres in a variety of habitats that include rough grassland, heaths, moors and sand dunes; it is also one of Orkney's commonest birds and can be found on all islands – a recent survey of Gairsay realised almost 30 pairs. In upland areas the unassuming Meadow Pipit becomes an important item in the diet of Kestrels, Merlins and Hen Harriers. However, unlike the Skylark, it is primarily insectivorous and finding suitable food in Orkney in winter is not an easy task. A handful of birds remain in the county but most of Orkney's breeding birds and their offspring head south in August and September; ringing has shown that many of them have arrived in Spain by late October. Travel can be swift; a North Ronaldsay bird caught and ringed on 29th September 1979 was in Badajoz in southwest Spain sixteen days later. Returning birds, often in sizeable flocks, appear in Orkney in late February or early March.

Dipper • Burns in spring and autumn; very hard to find

The fact that Dippers are not a regular feature of the Orkney landscape is surprising. In the United Kingdom, they are chiefly found on fast flowing stretches of water in mountainous and hilly districts and, across the Pentland Firth in Caithness and Sutherland, Dippers are frequent on the burns and rivers. In Orkney, there appear to be many suitable stretches of appropriate water, but the fact is, seeing Dippers is rare and seeing breeding Dippers is rarer still. The tumbling burns of Hoy have held Dippers in the past but the last breeding pair was in Rackwick in 1994 and that, apparently, the first since 1940. Like a large, black and white barrel-chested Wren, Dippers are truly aquatic and are able to feed and walk underwater. Their delightful bobbing and curtseying on boulders in mid-stream would be a welcome addition to Orkney's burns.

Dipper in May on Pegal Burn, Hoy with brig in the background.

Rock Pipit • *Tang Sparrow, Shore Sparrow* • Shore and cliffs all year; very easy to find

Many stretches of rocky shoreline in Orkney have a pair of resident Rock Pipits. They are widely distributed around the coasts of all the islands and in the main occupy a narrow feeding band extending from the low-tide mark to the cliff top; food preferences are for small marine molluscs, sand hoppers and flies. They are slightly larger and darker than their more widespread cousin, the Meadow Pipit, and show olive colouring in their feathering, long dark legs and smoky-grey outer tail feathers. The plaintive, almost insipid, call of the Meadow Pipit is replaced by an urgent and strident "*phist*" from its coastal counterpart. In spring and summer, male Rock Pipits perform a parachute display, spectacular in itself but doubly so against a roaring cliff updraught. The nest, which is never far from the sea (although could be 100 metres above it!), is usually well concealed on a ledge or in a cliff-face cleft. In wintertime, some birds vacate their normal strip of coast and are found in less than typical situations – birds are frequently located high in the peat hill and on one stormy winter's day I saw two searching the walls of the old Kirkwall Public Library in Laing Street. They can be found breeding on stretches of hard coast throughout the length of Britain's coastline and in wintertime can be located on soft coast as well.

Rock Pipit in May at the Haven, Swona – background, cliffs of South Ronaldsay with Barth Head to the right.

Yellow Wagtail with Blue-headed Wagtail on left in May at the Loch of Tankerness, St Andrews – background, the Glebe and St Andrews manse.

Yellow Wagtail • Wetlands and shore in spring and autumn; hard to find

There are six different races of the Yellow Wagtail in Europe and they come in a variety of stunning guises. All of them have buttercup yellow bellies and greenish mantles but their head and face patterns exhibit varying amounts of blue, black and white. However, the race that usually breeds in Britain, *"flavissima"*, is arguably the dullest of the group and lacks the "blue head" of its Continental cousin. Winter is spent in West Africa and by mid April the first returning birds reach the southern shores of Britain. They are primarily associated with freshwater and preferred habitats include damp cattle-grazed pastures, water meadows, marshy fields and sewage works. The meagre Scottish population in the south of the country is getting smaller and recent surveys indicate that its range within Britain continues to contract. The finger points to the draining of wet fields, the intensification of agriculture and the replacement of grasslands with cereals. Flies and spiders account for 80% of the Yellow Wagtail's diet and they like nothing better than a wet field full of cattle kicking up flies. Surprisingly, breeding has occurred in Orkney – Papa Westray in 1979 and Westray in 1980. They have a lyrical *"tswee"* call and passage birds, which can include "blue heads", are most likely to be encountered in wetlands or on the shore in May and September. North Ronaldsay seems to attract most of Orkney's Yellow Wagtails, but localities such as the Loch of Tankerness and the Loch of Graemeshall have also been frequented.

Grey Wagtail (male left, female right) in May on Mill Burn, Kirbister, Orphir – background, Kirbister Mill and brig.

Grey Wagtail • Burns in spring, summer, autumn and occasionally winter; hard to find

As a breeding bird, the Grey Wagtail is invariably associated with fast flowing freshwater, either along rocky, upland burns or at weirs and mill races on lowland rivers. Widely distributed in Britain, it is scarce in the flatter east and more numerous in the north and west except for the Outer Hebrides, Orkney and Shetland. With its chattering flight call, like two ball-bearings being knocked together, and its long-tailed bouncing flight, the Grey Wagtail is usually easy to locate. Their striking patterning includes white, grey, black and vivid yellow. Males, with their black throats, have underparts washed completely with sulphur; the female's undercarriage on the other hand is less yellow and the throat is pale. Eggs can be laid as early as March and the nest is nearly always above flowing water. A few pairs breed along Orkney's burns each summer and in recent years sites on Hoy and in Evie, Firth, Orphir and St Ola have been used. Upland areas are vacated as autumn approaches and most Grey Wagtails leave for southwest Britain and Ireland where they can be found on farms, at sewage works and in towns and gardens. Some venture even further afield with ultimate destinations in Spain, Portugal and North Africa. A few birds spend winter in Orkney and favoured sites include the Willow Burn in Kirkwall and the Ouse in Finstown.

Pied Wagtail • *Willie Wagtail* • Farms, wetlands and shore in spring, summer and autumn; very easy to find. Towns in winter; hard to find

Returning to Orkney in late February and early March, the appearance of Pied Wagtails helps to announce the lengthening of the day. With their striking pied plumage, bounding flight, "*chisick*" call and wagging tails they are easily identified. Previously uncommon, nowadays they are a familiar bird to most folk and occupy suitable sites throughout the isles; this recent increase in the county parallels a similar increase in the Outer Hebrides and Shetland. They breed in close proximity to man and as in the rest of Britain, most Orkney farms seem to have their pair of Pied Wagtails. They are also readily seen near roads where adjacent drystone dykes provide ample nest sites and the tarmac provides plenty of insects damaged by vehicles. In Britain they are ubiquitous in urban and rural habitats and breed everywhere except for woods and bare mountain and moorland. However, they are more abundant in the north and west where mixed farming and livestock help provide suitable habitat diversity. Although a handful of birds remain in Orkney over winter, most head south – lowland meadows, sewage farms, reservoirs and towns in Ireland, southern Britain and the Continent are popular

Pied Wagtail (female left, male right) in May at Midbea, Westray – background, North Midhouse and Fitty Hill.

destinations. On arriving and before leaving the islands, birds form nighttime roosts at localities such as Stromness Academy, Kirkwall Grammar School, Kirkwall marina and No 1 barrier. Later in the year, some of Orkney's birds may be part of the spectacular winter gatherings that collect in cities and towns – since 1929 there has been a roost in O'Connell Street in Dublin, which can number 3,000 birds.

White Wagtail • Shore in spring and autumn; hard to find

This is the Continental version of Britain's Pied Wagtail and breeds in most of Europe, Iceland and Shetland – it has also bred at least once in Orkney. It is frequently seen in the county especially at or near the coast and usually during April and May. Although very similar to its British cousin, look out for its pale grey mantle and the separated black cap and bib.

White Wagtail (male left, female right) in May at the Bay of Hinderayre, Rendall – (l-r) boathouses, old Rendall kirk and Gairsay.

Waxwing • Gardens in autumn, winter and spring; hard to find

With their crests, black masks, yellow-edged tail and red waxy blobs on their wings, Waxwings are one of our most spectacular garden visitors and a call from these exotic and entertaining arctic wanderers will never be forgotten. In most years a handful of birds appear in the county; indeed some town gardens blessed with bountiful crops of red berries are favoured annually. However, it is the large-scale arrivals, or irruptions, which catch our attention and become a talking point that enriches the dark winter days. Such is the interest generated that the irruptions often feature on the airwaves of local radio or in the columns of the press. Waxwings usually arrive in Britain after the Redwings and Fieldfares have stripped the countryside of berries; consequently, in their search for succulent red berries, Waxwings must descend on urban gardens and feed on the berries of cotoneaster and pyracanthus, the hips of roses and the pods of fuchsia. More recently, this urban specialist, has become known as the "supermarket bird"; almost indifferent to the presence of shoppers and their trolleys, they consume in bulk the tree fruits from the ornamental berried vegetation that now surrounds the large chain stores. What brings them to Britain in such numbers? Most usually it is due to a successful Waxwing breeding season and a poor crop of their staple food, the rowan berry. This lack of food means that they must travel across the Baltic and North Sea to seek adequate supplies of food. Consumption rates are quite staggering; birds have been observed eating as many as 600 berries in a six hour period. Occasionally, on calm autumn and winter days they can be seen catching flies; this may not be such a surprise when one realizes that during the summer in the far north, mosquitoes are their main food source.

Waxwings in December feeding on cotoneaster at 15.40 in Tankerness House Museum gardens, Kirkwall – background, museum and St Magnus Cathedral.

151

Wrens in June at the Hermitage of David Rawlings, Hamarfield, Rousay – (l-r)
Loch of Wasbister, Saviskaill Bay and Faraclett Head.

Wren • *Jenny Wren, Wirran, Wrannock* • Uplands, woodlands, scrub, gardens and coasts, all year; very easy to find

This bundle of brown and chestnut feathers and weighing no more than ten grams is the ultimate pocket dynamo, and is energy and vitality personified. It has an incredibly forceful presence and its song, which is with us for most of the year, is far-carrying and demands an audience. Often the first indication of its presence is the exuberant trill or scolding churr and rattle, the latter instantly conveying indignation at your presence. Its habitat requirements are different to other birds; it is found almost anywhere from sea-level to hill tops as long as crannies and crevices are plentiful; it is literally a troglodyte, (a cave dweller), and is able to forage for food and find shelter in sites that other birds find inaccessible. Orkney is no different and Wrens occur in most places, from thick hill heather to gardens and woodlands and from cliffs and shore to farm outbuildings and dykes – anywhere where spiders and insects can be located. Incredibly, they are able to exist below snow cover. With such an ability to adapt, it is not surprising that it is one of the most widespread species in Britain. Despite the bravado, Wrens are severely affected by hard weather and in harsh conditions, this normally anti-social bird will form impressive communal roosts in order to keep warm and survive cold spells. During one recent winter, 60 Wrens were seen to enter a tit nest box in Norfolk and 96 followed each other into the eaves of a house in Gloucestershire. The male can build up to ten nests for the female to choose from; in fact a bird in Holland was observed to build 40 in one year! The female's choice is normally the most cryptic and nests are renowned for the quirkiness of location – often cited is a nest in the mouth of a prized, wall-mounted, pike. Orkney's Wrens, like most of the species, are fairly sedentary. Research though has shown that birds move short distances locally in the county; so far the most adventurous individual yet discovered was a Rendall born bird that was retrapped during the following winter on Westray.

Dunnock • *Hemplie, Titling* • Woodlands, scrub and gardens all year; not easy to find

Some birds' names seem to be more apt than others – Dunnock is one of the apt ones. Literally meaning a small brown bird, outwardly the Dunnock appears shy, retiring and almost apologetic. In Orkney, it's probably most often seen in urban gardens hopping and shuffling along the ground underneath bird feeders, hedges and dykes, pecking at minute particles, and looking *almost* like a House Sparrow. However its mouse-like movements and solitariness are quite unlike the bouncy, chirpy sparrow-lifestyle and its subtle plumage tones are well-worth a second look. Most surprisingly, this outwardly unassuming guise hides a very complex social life in which monogamy is not the norm and where two males can share up to four females. Over a ten-day period, birds have been observed mating once or twice per hour, so much for being shy and retiring! In Orkney they are certainly not common, but in springtime they are easier to see, often choosing high and prominent perches from which to sing their thin, warbling song that can be heard from gardens in the towns and villages, woodlands, willow and gorse scrub. Nests are located in thick low vegetation, often ivy, nettles or brambles, and up to five stunning blue eggs are incubated. In Britain, while shunning high ground, the Dunnock is a widespread and common bird, and a key player in the urban environment. In general they are sedentary birds rarely moving more than a few kilometres from their breeding sites. Continental birds, however, behave differently; first of all they are less of a garden bird and tend to favour scrubby hillside woodland. Secondly they migrate, and in autumn, Dunnocks from Scandinavia can be found along Orkney's eastern shores – their single-note and high-pitched call usually reveals their presence before they are seen.

Dunnocks during early spring in Gyre Wood, Orphir.

Robin • *Robin Redbreast* • Coasts in spring and autumn, gardens and woodlands all year; easy to find

In some years, especially in autumn, Robins can be very numerous in Orkney. Easterly winds carry Continental Robins across the North Sea, and a walk along any eastern shore in the county will often yield these woodland birds searching for insects and shelter in geos, eager to replenish their energy reserves. No doubt some of these birds remain in Orkney but ringing has shown that many may journey as far as northern France before attempting to fly back, often via Orkney, to their Scandinavian breeding grounds in spring. Robins can be widespread in the county towards the end of the year; their insistent ticking call and their melancholy song are often unexpected but welcome additions to a calm and clear autumnal Orkney evening. There is a small breeding population that may be found nesting in gardens in the towns and villages, in woodlands and in willow scrub in upland localities, but the emphasis is on the word small; Orkney's most extensive broad-leaved woodland, Binscarth, is home to probably no more than three or four pairs. Young birds look quite unlike their parents; they lack the red breast – in its place is a mottled brown and buff waistcoat. With a diet of chiefly ground-living prey a prolonged fall of snow may result in heavy mortality. Throughout most of mainland Britain, Robins are one of the most widely distributed and abundant birds and are found in all types of woodland, hedgerows, parks and gardens.

Left: Robin during winter in Franklin Road, Stromness – (l-r) M.V.Hamnavoe, Hoy high, Graemsay and Stromness Town Hall.

Centre: Robin (juvenile) in July in the garden of The Lieutenant's House, Ferry Road, Stromness.

Bluethroat (male) in May at the old Public Hall, Rothiesholm, Stronsay with Spurness turbines, Sanday in the background.

Bluethroat • Coasts and scrub in spring and autumn; very hard to find

The red-spotted form breeds in the far northern latitudes of Scandinavia, Russia and now the Yukon in Canada. It is this form that appears most frequently in Orkney. Easterly winds and rain in spring and autumn are likely to deposit these red-tailed jewels on to Orkney's eastern coasts where they can be found scurrying and foraging mouse-like on the ground. Birch and willow scrub areas with nearby running water are typical breeding sites. Similar locations occur in Scotland and pairs bred in 1968 and 1995; in Orkney during the early summer of 1981 a male sang in Birsay but unfortunately failed to attract a like-minded female.

Redstart • Coasts and scrub in spring and autumn; hard to find

Usually the first indication of a Redstart is the flash of a red tail as it disappears over a dyke – most views tend to be rear views! In Orkney it is most likely to be seen in the autumn on the coast. A combination of easterly winds and rain as Scandinavian birds migrate to West Africa, can result in large numbers (a "fall"), arriving on the county's eastern coasts to seek shelter and food. One of the most remarkable "falls" occurred in September 1965 along the length of Britain's east coast but most dramatically in Suffolk. On a two-mile walk near Walberswick in Suffolk, 15,000 Redstarts were encountered and a similar number were estimated at the Minsmere RSPB reserve. Nothing quite like that has occurred in Orkney in recent years but it is not unusual for as many as 20 to be recorded on North Ronaldsay, Sanday or Stronsay on a late autumn day. They also occur in spring in much fewer numbers; it is in April and May when the stunning plumage of the male is best seen. Given that they spend their creative summers in woodlands, hedgerows, orchards and parks, they must find Orkney an unnerving place to be. In Britain they are essentially a bird of the western oak woods where they tend to inhabit the clearings, rides and edges. Breeding as far north as the woods of Sutherland, they are absent as nesting birds from the treeless outer islands.

Redstarts (male left, female right) in May at the Brough of Deerness, Deerness – background, the Horse of Copinsay and Copinsay.

Black Redstart • Coasts in spring and autumn; very hard to find

Just like its close relative the Redstart, it's the glimpse of red tail that usually gives the Black Redstart away. It is most likely to be seen in the county during spring and autumn when European birds are in the throes of migration and easterly winds and rain have deposited them in small numbers around Orkney's coasts. Possibly it was after such conditions that a pair decided to remain on Copinsay in 1973; eggs were laid and this constituted the first nesting record for Scotland. Black Redstarts are intriguing birds. On the Continent they tend to be mountain birds using boulder strewn slopes and scree; in Britain derelict sites mimicked this habitat and the first regular breeding commenced on the derelict Wembley exhibition site in the 1920s. More suitable breeding sites were made available following the bombing of London in the 1940s and to this day the southeast of England remains the breeding stronghold. Following the redevelopment of bombed sites, Black Redstarts have become birds of large buildings – power stations, cathedrals, warehouses and even palaces have been used. There are probably no more than 100 pairs in Britain, but some may go unnoticed given their choice to breed in unattractive locations, which may be avoided by birdwatchers.

Black Redstarts (male left, female right) in May at Burwick farm, South Ronaldsay with Burwick pier in the background.

Stonechat • Coastal and upland scrub all year; easy to find

For most of the year, Stonechats make themselves highly visible and highly audible. In spring and summer, they are inquisitive, extrovert, bold and all too willing to scold your presence. A walk in areas of coastal or hill heather where there is also willow scrub, will often witness the antics of these neat and colourful insect eaters, and their frequent use of high perches, be it bushes, fence posts or electricity wires, makes for relatively easy observation. In the autumn they can be even easier to see. Family parties, some of which may be migrating, can be wide-ranging and often forsake their typical habitat, turning up in rural gardens and set-aside fields. Being an insectivore means that harsh winters are challenging and it is then that they become less than easy to find; possibly many of Orkney's breeding birds leave the county for a warmer clime, one which provides a plentiful supply of insects. The county's population is restricted to a core on Hoy and the West Mainland and a handful of pairs on Rousay and Eday. The effect of harsh winters may result in a contraction of its range, while a succession of mild winters may see an increase of breeding birds in suitable habitats in parishes and islands. In Britain they are primarily found in the south and west, some in upland areas but more typically in coastal areas where there is gorse, heather or bracken. The breeding season is long; singing is often heard in February and birds, even in Orkney, may have three broods. During winter, freezing conditions can spell disaster; thus many of Britain's birds, if not already there, move to the coast – some in fact journey to the Mediterranean. With his jet-black head, white collar and wing panels, and orange breast, the male makes a bold statement; the female is more subdued and lacks the black head and white collar.

Left: Stonechats (juvenile on left, female in the middle and male on right) in April at St Mary's kirk, Eday.

Whinchats (male left, female right) in May at Hackland, Rendall – background, old Hackland kirk and Enyas Hill.

Whinchat • Coasts and scrub in spring and autumn; hard to find

Across the Pentland Firth in western Caithness and Sutherland, Whinchats, as a breeding bird, are not that uncommon. The same cannot be said for Orkney where examples are rare. Melsetter and Berriedale on Hoy, held pairs in the 19th century and since then there have been a handful of breeders on Hoy and in Rendall, the last in 1995. They are similar to Stonechats; they are insectivores, they utilise prominent perches from which to catch insect prey and their preferred habitat is rough ground, usually consisting of gorse, heathland and tussocky grass. In appearance, they are alike being of comparable size and washed with the same colours. Plumage-wise, the big difference is that Whinchats have a prominent buff supercilium and a buff moustachial stripe. The other major distinction is their lifestyles; in general Stonechats are sedentary but Whinchats migrate. After a winter in Africa, they return to Britain in April and May. Breeding numbers have diminished over the last century due to the loss of suitable habitat in lowland areas. A tidier Britain, with for example frequently mown roadside verges, has resulted in a retreat to higher ground. During spring and autumn migrations, Orkney's eastern coastlines are frequently visited by off course Continental birds.

Wheatear • *Stonechat, Chuckie, Stinkie-buil, Chacko* • Upland
stony slopes and coasts in spring, summer and autumn; easy to find

Newly arrived in March and April, fresh-plumaged spring birds look stunning. Following the greyness of winter, their appearance is a tonic; it's as though we have forgotten that such vibrant colours exist. Their behaviour is uplifting; they dash, stop, bob, bow, wing flick, tail wag, tail spread and then fly to a perch to repeat the bobbing and bowing; each time they move the brightness and whiteness of their rumps dazzles. In Orkney during spring they arrive on any of the county's coasts before making their way to their summer territories. They are birds of open stony country and a combination of short-cropped turf for feeding, and old buildings, dykes, heaps of stones and rabbit burrows for nesting is the ideal. Some of the most frequently used areas in Orkney are the maritime heaths of the West Mainland, Rousay and Westray. Their winter is spent in North Africa in areas of desert not dissimilar to the stone-strewn turf in western Orkney. In Britain they are mainly found in the north and west and their loud chacking calls and rather unmusical but lively song is characteristic of upland areas. Not so long ago, they were abundant over lowland Britain and along the southern coasts of England and thousands were caught to please the palates of gourmets. Daniel Defoe described them as "the most delicious taste for a creature of one mouthful". However, since those days of plenty, much downland has been ploughed and afforested and grazing, whether by sheep or rabbit,

has been reduced, the latter by myxomatosis; consequently, Wheatears have retreated to high ground. The male, with his bandit-like black mask and blue grey cloak, is easily separated from the warm, orange and buff female.

Greenland Wheatear • Coasts in spring and autumn; not easy to find and be certain of

This distinctive race *(leucorhoa)*, which breeds in Iceland, Greenland and eastern Canada, is bigger, bolder and brighter than our usual Wheatears and arrives on our shores slightly later. They are approximately 15% larger, have richer and more uniformly coloured underparts and stand more upright on longer legs.

Left: Wheatears (female left, male right) in June at Forcewell, Yesnaby, Sandwick with Brough of Bigging in the background.

Greenland Wheatear (male) in June at Rerwick, St Andrews – background, Shapinsay Sound and Shapinsay.

Ring Ouzel • *Flitterchack, Hill Chack* • Upland gorges, coasts and sometimes rural gardens in spring and autumn; hard to find

It is a real pity that in Orkney we don't hear the fluty song, penetrating whistles and stony "chacking" of Ring Ouzels more frequently. These shy, unapproachable and flighty thrushes nearly always nest in upland areas that contain crags and bushes. It would appear that the right sort of habitat exists in Orkney especially on Hoy, Rousay and in the West Mainland hills and it is in these areas where the few instances of breeding or suspected breeding have occurred. Across the Pentland Firth, Ring Ouzels can be found in the hills of Sutherland and Caithness but it appears that all but the most intrepid birds are content to remain on the British mainland; the last confirmed Orkney breeding record was of a pair on Hoy on 1977. In Britain Ring Ouzels have undergone a decline in the last hundred years. The reasons are probably many but this shy bird is possibly more susceptible than some to increased recreational disturbance from activities such as hill walking and hang gliding. It has also been suggested that the spread of Blackbirds from the lowlands into the highlands in the United Kingdom has resulted in the displacement of its mountain cousin. Outwardly both male and female Ring Ouzels have very similar plumage to Blackbirds; subtly different is the amount of white seen on the fringes of both the wing feathers and the body feathers, which is noticeable both at rest and in flight. However, the most obvious plumage difference is the Ring Ouzel's gorget, in the male it is strikingly white, the female's is more subdued. Passage birds can be found around Orkney's eastern coasts in spring and more especially autumn; an exceptional influx took place on 27 October 1976 when over 100 North Africa bound birds were located in Kirkwall's gardens.

Ring Ouzels (female left, male right) in May at the Burn of Berri Dale, Hoy.

Blackbirds, (young on the left, female in the middle, male on the right) during July in Balfour village, Shapinsay.

Blackbird • *Blackie, Chucket* • Gardens, woodlands and coasts all year; very easy to find

Nowadays Blackbirds are one of our most familiar birds. They are the adaptable member of the thrush family and are found throughout Britain and Ireland in a variety of habitats from suburban parks and gardens to woodlands, farmland and moorland edge. Virtually the only areas avoided are high and bare mountain. However, they haven't always been so widespread. In the very distant past, Blackbirds were most likely found purely in deep forest; the plumage of both cock and hen parallels some of the world's tropical thrushes and their low fluty song is appropriate for forest life. It appears that since medieval times Blackbirds have adapted to a more catholic lifestyle and with recent climatic amelioration, have extended their geographical range, which has included spreads in Scandinavia and Ireland and the colonization of Shetland, the Faeroes and the Azores – however, they are not yet established in Iceland. In Orkney, they can be found almost everywhere but are most evident in gardens, be it town, village or country and with the recent increase in woodland planting, it is likely that Orkney Blackbirds will increase. Their songs are liquid and melodic, their alarm calls can smack of hysteria. Nests are often located in low bushes and it is not unusual to find them in man-made locations. They are also very numerous on passage; birds visiting Orkney in spring are usually on their way back to Scandinavia, central Europe and Russia while autumn birds, sometimes in exceptionally large gatherings, are heading southwest, many to Ireland, fleeing the onset of the Continental winter. It's easy to separate the males from the females, the males are black and the females are brown. Furthermore, males without a bright yellow/orange beak are young males.

Song Thrush • *Mavis* • Coasts in spring and autumn, gardens all year; not easy to find

Even as early as January, the short winter days are brightened up by the song of the Song Thrush. Usually delivered from a lofty perch and often after a period of rain, its repetitive phrases are bold and clear. In Orkney, Song Thrushes are fairly widespread, although never common, and breed in the gardens of the towns and villages and in the woodlands. The nest, which is mud lined, is usually built within a metre of the ground. As in the rest of Britain, Orkney's breeding Song Thrushes have declined; there were considered to be 18 territories in Berstane woods in 1975, nowadays, it is doubtful if there are that number of territories throughout Kirkwall and Stromness. The decline has been due to a combination of factors one of which is the Song Thrushes' susceptibility to harsh weather. This is clearly illustrated by the Shetland experience; until the extremely fierce winter of 1946/47, up to two dozen pairs bred there, now there are none. Song Thrushes have also witnessed a loss of feeding opportunities. With the switch to autumn sown cereals and the subsequent loss of tilled land in spring, insects to feed youngsters have been in shorter supply. Furthermore, the increased use of garden pesticides has reduced the availability of snails and in both summer and winter, this food resource has always been one of the most important items of its diet. British Song Thrushes are warm brown, Continental Song Thrushes are slightly larger and greyer-brown; during the autumn, it is possible to see these birds around Orkney's eastern coasts. Ringing has demonstrated that some of these migrants are heading as far south as Iberia or North Africa.

Song Thrush in March at Water Gate, Kirkwall – (l-r) the Olde Manse, the Bishop's Palace, St Magnus Cathedral and the former Police Station.

Fieldfare • Short grasslands and woodlands in autumn, winter and spring; easy to find

In Orkney, it is during autumn, more especially October, when you are most likely to bump into these heralds of winter. Summer is spent nesting in Scandinavia and Russia. The rowan berry is the staple food for both youngsters and adults and the abundance of the crop determines their winter schedule – a poor crop means mass migration. In fact, in some years, Orkney can witness exceptionally large arrivals of these big, grey-headed northern thrushes; such can be the volume of birds that fields of short grass turn into moving carpets. As they forage restlessly and scour the turf for insects, they give the impression that this autumn visit will be brief and that there is a further, distant destination, in which they will spend the winter. Often within a few days they have gone, many to spend the winter in the mildness of Ireland. Later in the year, a few more birds may arrive in Orkney often to eke an existence from the handouts of berries from ornamental shrubs in the town gardens. Once these supplies are exhausted, these highly nomadic birds move on. Studies have shown that birds seen in Britain in October may travel as far afield as Greece or Portugal in search of their winter sustenance. They can be colonial, nesting in a wide variety of habitats – everything from parks, gardens and plantations to willow scrub, moorland valleys and even above the tree line – often they are found close to water. They rarely breed in Britain and it was in 1967 that Happy Valley in Stenness was home to Britain's first known Fieldfare nest. Their plumage features a combination of pearly grey, black and rufous and in flight their silvery-white underwings and grey rumps are most noticeable • in Spain they are known as the royal thrush. The chattering chacking call is a brisk and crisp sound of autumn heard as loose migrating flocks pass overhead.

Redwing • *Windthrush* • Short grasslands and woodlands in autumn, winter and spring; easy to find

This is the smallest of our regular thrushes. Their demeanour and plumage are sharp, quite different to the rounded brown-ness of a Song Thrush and they are a fraction tinier. They have rusty red flanks, which can vary in intensity, and the red (as in

Fieldfare in October at The Glebe, St Andrews.

Redwings in November near the Knowes of Esco, Quoys, Sandwick.

Redwing) is on the underside of their wings and is only seen when in flight. It is the horizontal stripe above the eye, which is their most distinctive plumage feature. Just like Fieldfares, Redwings are at their most numerous during October when gatherings from Scandinavia, Russia, central Europe and Iceland stop off briefly in Orkney on their way to their winter food supplies which may be as far afield as Iberia. They are very nomadic and move large distances in response to poor weather and available food. An individual ringed on South Ronaldsay in October 1993 was found in south central Portugal just 28 days later. In some years flocks are vast; in 1976 up to 70,000 birds were estimated over Kirkwall and in the following year 10,000 roosted in Berstane Woods. During their stay in the county they are most likely to be found either foraging for invertebrates in the open fields in the company of Starlings and Fieldfares, or feeding on fruit or turning leaf litter in gardens. Their presence can also be detected at night when their high-pitched and thin calls cut through the darkness. As a breeding bird, Redwings can be found nesting near willow and birch scrub in Europe's northern latitudes. They also breed in Britain and are relatively new additions; the first instance of nesting was in Sutherland as recently as 1925 but since then they have secured a firm hold especially in the northwest of Scotland where they breed in a wide variety of woodland habitats often close to running water. In Orkney their piercing and fluty song is often heard in spring and in some years pairs have been tempted to stay; in 1975 a pair bred in Orphir and in 1993 a pair was unsuccessful on Stronsay. However, despite frequent instances of birds in song, these remain the only Orkney examples.

Mistle Thrush • Uplands and woodlands in spring; very hard to find

It has never been adequately explained and still remains a mystery why the Mistle Thrush increased so rapidly in Britain in the 18th and 19th centuries. What we do know is that prior to this it was chiefly a bird of European mountain forests. The change is well illustrated by Ireland's experience – the first bird occurred in 1800 and by mid century they were resident countrywide. In a very short period of time, from being a shy bird of the mountains it had become one able to live in proximity to man. It appears to thrive where there is a combination of woodland edge and open country; this includes suburban parks with surrounding playing fields and lawns. Berry bearing trees and shrubs such as holly, yew, hawthorn and in Europe, mistletoe (from which its name derives) are important food resources especially through the winter and defended aggressively. Although Mistle Thrushes have never been numerous, this expansion was also witnessed in Orkney. Birds nested at Westness on Rousay and in Kirkwall during the mid 19th century, while, seemingly, in the first half of the 20th century, Mistle Thrushes were not uncommon; the woodlands of Balfour, Berstane and Binscarth all held breeding pairs. A decrease followed, the last nesting attempt occurred in Kirkwall in 1972. Nowadays, this large, grey, boldly-spotted and wild thrush with its rattling call is known solely as a bird of passage, chiefly occurring in March and April.

Mistle Thrush in March at Russadale quarry, Stenness.

Sedge Warbler • Lowland freshwater with scrub in spring, summer and autumn; easy to find

As warblers go, the Sedge is one of the easiest to identify and also one of the easiest to find. Between May and August, Sedge Warblers can be found among patches of iris, willow, canary grass and reed in lowland areas of all Orkney's large islands. The first indication of their presence is usually the song, which is far-carrying and has been described variously as "vigorous bouts of cheerful chatter" and "hectic and magical". Study has determined that each bird's song is unique and each performance is unique; many phrases within the song imitate other birds that the Sedge Warbler is in contact with such as Reed Bunting, Swallow and Pied Wagtail. They can also be very visible; their display flight involves a chattering ascent before spiralling down on outspread wings. Songs are often delivered from conspicuous perches when the giveaway creamy-white supercilium is easily seen. Apparently Orkney was colonised in the mid 19th century and now represents Britain's northernmost outpost. Ringing has illustrated that individuals are extremely faithful to their nest sites and many birds have been retrapped in the same Orkney locality year after year. Elsewhere in Britain it is widely distributed in lowland areas with East Anglia being a particular stronghold. Winter is spent in West Africa where drought conditions can affect survival and consequently the numbers of returning birds in spring.

Icterine Warbler • Coasts, scrub and woodlands in spring and autumn; very hard to find

This heavy-billed, upright and pale yellow warbler, which looks like many others of its family, comes from eastern and central Europe where it is a bird of towns and gardens. Easterly winds in spring and autumn usually mean that a few individuals are seen in Orkney each year and occasionally spring birds are heard to sing. In 2002 a surprising event occurred on Stronsay; a pair nested, only the second time ever in Scotland.

Top: Sedge Warbler in May at Russland Mill, Harray.

Icterine Warbler in July 2002 at the Mill, Stronsay.

Blackcap • Coasts, gardens and woodlands in spring and autumn, gardens in winter; not easy to find

The black-capped male and the brown-capped female have become quite familiar autumn and winter birds in Orkney's gardens. This hasn't always been the case – in the last one hundred years these migrants, mostly from Scandinavia, the Low Countries and central and eastern Europe, have become increasingly common in Britain. There was an average of barely more than 20 birds per winter in the 1940s and 1950s. Now, possibly because of all our bird feeders and tables, thousands spend winter in the UK. These particular birds are totally different to the ones that breed in Britain; the British birds spend the winter in·the western Mediterranean, trying to avoid the guns and traps of hunters and the knives and forks of restaurants. On returning in March and April, if insects are scarce, they feed on ivy berries. Though scarce in the Highlands and absent from higher ground, they are widespread in lowland mature woods. They have a loud and rich song hence its other names: "*mock Nightingale*", "*northern Nightingale*" and "*March Nightingale*". It has nested just a few times in Orkney; the most likely places for nesting are to be found in the larger woodlands.

Garden Warbler • Coasts and scrub in spring and autumn; not easy to find

Easterly winds in spring and autumn occasion the arrival of these rather nondescript birds to Orkney's eastern fringes. They are closely related to Blackcaps and their breeding habitats, songs and looks are similar. Heavy-bodied and stubby-billed they are best recognised by their absence of striking features although their big round eyes and smooth head impart a look of gentleness. As a breeding bird in Britain they are less widespread than Blackcaps and tend to prefer scrubbier woodlands. Garden Warblers have bred on a couple of occasions in Orkney; in the 1960s a pair nested in successive years in Binscarth Wood. After the breeding season, Central Africa is their winter destination.

Top: Blackcaps (female left, male right) in September at St Mary's kirk, Burwick, South Ronaldsay.

Garden Warbler in August at Fersness quarry, Eday.

Barred Warbler in October at Newark chapel, Deerness with Newark Bay in the background.

Barred Warbler • Coasts and scrub in autumn; very hard to find

This, one of Europe's largest warblers, nests among scrub bushes in open areas across eastern and central Europe. In autumn, easterly winds carry them to Britain where they are found chiefly on the east coast. In Orkney they occur with regularity in the autumn especially along the North Sea coasts. They are big and unlike some of their daintier warbler cousins crash around the bushes in a clumsy and gung-ho manner.

Chiffchaff in April at Graemeshall, Holm.

Chiffchaff • Coasts, woodlands and gardens in spring, autumn and occasionally winter; not easy to find

On a sun-bright April morning nothing gladdens the heart or dispels the grey-gloom of winter more than the insistent and repetitive song of this tiny warbler. Perched on top of a still-leafless but leaf-budding tree, the Chiffchaff's *"chiff chaff, chiff chaff"* song, is one of the easiest to recognise. Many of Britain's birds have spent the winter in West Africa; by early April they are back at their breeding sites which are chiefly old deciduous woodlands with tall trees for song posts and dense undergrowth for nesting. They are found over much of southern Britain; in Scotland they are more thinly spread and have a preference for large gardens or woodlands that include rhododendrons. Although their song is heard frequently in Orkney during the spring and nesting has been suspected, there has been only one confirmed instance of breeding – a pair at Trumland on Rousay during 2001. Like the Blackcap, the number of Chiffchaffs spending the winter in Britain is increasing and, again like the Blackcap, many of them are Continental birds which move west to Britain's milder winter climate. However, unlike the Blackcap and its preference for bird table food, the Chiffchaff remains an insectivorous bird during the winter. Surviving in Orkney may be difficult on such a diet and consequently, most birds gravitate to the comparative shelter provided by town gardens.

Whitethroat and Lesser Whitethroat in September at the Covenanter's Memorial, Deerness with the Mull Head in the background.

176

Whitethroat • Coasts and scrub in spring and autumn; hard to find

This, like its close cousin the Lesser Whitethroat, is a bird of hedges, scrub, young forestry plantations and overgrown gardens. In fact Whitethroats have an enduring link with hedges and benefited greatly from the 18th century enclosure acts. Up until the 1960s, although shunning higher ground, it was considered to be the most generally distributed of the warblers that bred in Britain and could be found nesting over much of England, Wales, lowland Scotland and Ireland. However in the spring of 1969, three quarters of Britain's breeding Whitethroats failed to reappear following a winter of drought in the Sahel region of Africa. Since then there have been further winter droughts and from a position of being very common in Britain, Whitethroats have become, in a few years, very uncommon. As with other summer migrants, easterly winds bring Whitethroats to Orkney's shores in spring and autumn. Occasionally some of the spring birds have stayed and bred; instances of nesting have occurred recently in Rendall, Firth, Stenness, St Ola and on South Ronaldsay. With its cheerful and chattering song flight, obtrusive scolding of intruders and glaring expression, Whitethroats make themselves obvious. They are less neatly marked than Lesser Whitethroats but their rusty-edged wings make identification fairly easy.

Lesser Whitethroat • Coasts and scrub in spring and autumn; hard to find

In Scotland, this is not a common breeding bird. The United Kingdom lies at the western edge of its European range and the majority of Britain's nesting birds occur in the south where its short, dry and rattling song is heard from English and Welsh hedgerows, overgrown gardens and scrub vegetation on chalk downs. However towards the end of the 20th century, breeding birds have become far more frequent in Scotland especially on the east coast south of the kingdom of Fife. In fact there have been a few instances of breeding further north and even in Orkney where nesting took place in 1988 at Holland House on North Ronaldsay in 1988 and in 2004 in Finstown. They are smart and jaunty looking birds; their clean pale underparts contrast sharply with their crisp white throats, lead grey upperparts and distinctive black bandit masks. Easterly winds in spring and autumn can bring many off course Lesser Whitethroats to the county's eastern coasts.

Willow Warbler • Coasts, scrub and woodlands in spring, summer and autumn; not easy to find

It wasn't until the 19th century that Willow Warblers and Chiffchaffs were separated as different species. They are very alike. The best way of separating them is to hear their song; the Chiffchaff's monotonous and repetitive song is so different to the Willow Warbler's descending cadence that covers a full octave. However if silent birds are met with, the Willow Warbler can usually be identified by its yellow-green plumage and pale legs that differ from the dull, grey-green plumage and dark legs of the Chiffchaff. In Britain Willow Warblers are considered to be the most widely distributed of our summer migrants. After a winter in Africa, they return to nest most numerously in young woods and scrub. They are absent from treeless high ground, islands and, unlike the Chiffchaff, they tend not to choose mature trees. Orkney may have been colonised in the 19th century; certainly by the 1940s they were considered to be in all the existing woodlands such as Berriedale, Binscarth, Balfour Castle and Trumland. With the recent surge in tree planting in the county, it is likely that Willow Warblers will find more sites to their liking. In spring and autumn, wayfaring migrants are likely to be seen on Orkney's eastern shores.

Willow Warbler during May at Trumland House gardens, Rousay.

Yellow-browed Warbler in October at Aikerskaill, Deerness.

Yellow-browed Warbler • Coasts and scrub in autumn and very occasionally spring; very hard to find

These waifs from Siberia are never common but can usually be guaranteed in Orkney along the eastern margins every autumn. They are birds of open hill, mountain and riverine scrub and should be spending the winter in southeast Asia. However, catching the wrong winds can send them spiralling to the other side of the world. The arrival of these delightfully pretty warblers, one of the birdwatcher's autumn highlights, is tinged with the sad realisation that they are very unlikely to find their way home and will ultimately perish on unfamiliar soil or over unfamiliar seas. They are a fraction smaller than either the Chiffchaff or Willow Warbler but are far more striking and colourful. Their green plumage seems warmer and richer and the broad yellow stripe above the eye and the double yellow bars on the wings make these warblers noticeably different.

Goldcrest • Coasts in spring and autumn, gardens and woodlands all year; not easy to find

It is Britain's smallest bird and one of the world's smallest, barely weighing more than 5 grams, the weight of a small coin. There are true stories of birds caught on flypapers (it happened in the Rendall shop!) and burdock heads. Yet the Goldcrest always appears bold in the presence of humans and is able to withstand northern winters of just six hours daylight and numbing temperatures of -25° C. In autumn, and occasionally spring, when easterly airflows displace Continental birds from their normal routes, it can be a very familiar and common bird in Orkney. Ringed birds have landed on Orkney shores from Norway, Sweden and quite incredibly the Czech Republic. However the pleasure in seeing such numbers can be tempered when witnessing its struggle and obvious frailty in hostile conditions. Typically they are breeding

Goldcrests (female left, male right) in April in the Sutherland plantation, Flotta – (l-r) WWII cinema, M.V.Hoy Head and Sutherland Pier.

birds of coniferous woodland and their increase in Britain has been due to new coniferous plantations – they can be found now even in the Isles of Scilly and Shetland. In conifers they have little competition for food and feed on small items that are unsuitable for other birds. Orkney's Goldcrests breed in the conifer plantations of Hoy, Flotta, Eday and the Mainland and their thin, tinkling song is usually the only sound you can hear in spring and early summer from these dark and silent places. Their nests are well insulated feather-lined cups crafted from moss, lichen and spiders webs. In wintertime the same sites can be alive with their high-pitched calls, and their confiding nature means that close encounters are frequent. They have a white wing bar, a beady eye and a head stripe of burnished gold for the male and lemon yellow for the female.

Spotted Flycatcher • Coasts, scrub, gardens and woodlands in spring and autumn; hard to find

This is a grey brown bird. Their plumage is often described as drab and bird books use adjectives such as "dull" or "mousey-grey". There is nothing showy about their appearance; the most that can be said is that they have a streaked breast and a peaked and streaked crown – "Streaked Flycatcher" would be more appropriate than "Spotted". Neither is their song spectacular; adjectives such as "thin" or "squeaky" are used. However these apparent deficiencies are countered by its confiding nature and aerobatic forays. Its hunting mode is an aerial ballet and these elegant moves are often accompanied by clicking sounds caused by its bill snapping closed as it snatches flying prey. They are birds of mature woodland, preferring glades and edges, but are also found in gardens, orchards and churchyards. Winter is spent in tropical Africa and they are one of the last migrants to arrive in Britain; their late arrival is dictated by the abundance and availability of the type of insects on which they feed. Unfortunately their fortunes have been affected and a decline, probably attributable to the use of pesticides, has been noted. Spotted Flycatchers occasionally, choose to nest in Orkney. This is not an annual event but breeding pairs have been seen at Melsetter, Binscarth, Balfour and Trumland in recent years. As with many other migrants, suitable spring and autumn weather conditions mean there is a chance of seeing flycatchers on eastern shores.

Spotted Flycatcher in June at the Gut of Carpaquoy, Eday – (l-r) Carpaquoy, Fall of Warness and Muckle Green Holm.

Pied Flycatcher • Coasts, scrub, gardens and woodlands in spring and autumn; hard to find

Of the two flycatchers that occur most frequently in Orkney, the Pied's plumage is far more obvious and makes for easier identification than the Spotted. The male is black and white; the upperparts are black and the white occurs on the belly and as a broad panel on the wing. The female or young male is less striking; the upperparts are brown, the underparts off-white and the white wing panel less extensive. In some years, during spring and autumn, they can be found on fence lines or in scrubland especially in the east of the county. Occasionally they may filter inland and be seen in gardens and it is their characteristic sallies from perches in search of insects that catch the eye. It is unlikely that they have ever bred in Orkney although there is a 19th century record from Melsetter. As breeding birds they are mostly found in the oak woods of western Britain where there are abundant perches and holes for nesting and a plentiful supply of flies and caterpillars to feed their young. Where natural nest sites are in short supply, they have taken to nest boxes with great enthusiasm.

Pied Flycatchers (male on left, female on right) in October at Cara, South Ronaldsay.

183

Top: Red-backed Shrikes (male left, female right) in June at the Stone of Setter, Eday – (l-r) Red Head, Carrick House and Grey Head.

Great Grey Shrike in October at St Lawrence's kirk, Burray with Copinsay in the background.

Red-backed Shrike • Coasts in spring and autumn; very hard to find

Barely 100 years ago Red-backed Shrikes were numerous and fairly widespread in Britain but even then ornithologists had detected a nationwide decline. In 1952 there was an estimated

300 pairs, in 1971 there were 80. Quite unexpectedly during this overall British decline, several pairs nested in Scotland in the 1970s and the unexpected included pairs on Hoy in 1970 and Firth in 1977. However, the optimism was short-lived and in 1989, for the very first time in ornithological history, Red-backed Shrikes did not breed in Britain. Nowadays, an occasional pair may nest, but they are to all intents and purposes extinct as a breeding bird. In their days of abundance they could be found anywhere that provided thorny bushes to build nests in and where a plentiful supply of prey could be impaled. Gardens, orchards and heathlands were favoured but as their numbers dwindled their preferred choice was heath with a mixture of gorse, heather and small pools and their strongholds became East Anglia and the New Forest. A number of reasons have been put forward for their decline including a loss of habitat, climate change, range contraction and egg collecting – eggers have always been attracted to Red-backed Shrikes because of the almost infinite variety of colours shown in their eggs. They have been likened to small fierce hawks and their thorn larders are draped with such items as bees, moths, beetles, birds, mammals and young snakes – little wonder they are also known as "*butcher*" birds (their Latin name *Lanio* means "I tear"!). Females and youngsters are a mixture of warm browns; the male, with a striking combination of grey head, chestnut back, pink breast and black mask is stunning. In Orkney, migrant birds are frequently seen in spring along eastern coasts.

Great Grey Shrike • Coasts in spring and autumn; very hard to find

In winter or summer, they are found in open country liberally dotted with convenient hunting perches. By all accounts, Great Grey Shrikes are considered to be even more rapacious than Red-backed Shrikes and prey items at butchering sites include insects, mammals as large as stoats and birds as big as grouse. They breed over much of central and eastern Europe and have never nested in Britain; however these striking black, grey and white birds are frequently seen in spring, more frequently in autumn and some even spend the winter here – on average 150 per year. On arrival along Britain's coast in autumn, these strongly territorial birds soon scatter and set up large, fiercely defended, hunting areas. Groundwater considered it to be the commonest of the shrikes in Orkney. Single birds are usually found in April or more often October along the county's eastern shores but rarely stay for long periods; there have been no instances of overwintering in Orkney.

Starling • *Stare, Stroling, Strill, Scootie* • Everywhere in town, coast and country all year; very easy to find

Up until the 20th century, Starlings were uncommon breeding birds in Britain and could only be found in the far north and west of Scotland. Essentially they were winter visitors from Europe and Russia; the Welsh name "*Aderyn yr Eira*" means snowbird and their arrival was seen as a sign of impending snow. They are social birds – this is most apparent in winter when large intense flocks scour pastureland and spectacular gatherings assemble prior to roosting. These large pre-roost flocks are exhilarating to watch as they twist, turn and tumble in breathtaking synchronicity. Above many of Britain's large towns Starling shows were a nightly feature and roosting birds would be packed shoulder to shoulder on the ledges of buildings. In 1949, the weight of roosting birds on the hands of Big Ben stopped the clock. Health and safety issues in towns have forced Starlings to find alternative roosting sites such as trees, reed beds and cliffs. In Orkney winter roosts can be found in all these places and also on the "Reginald", a blockship off the 3rd barrier. Ringing has shown that these roosts are composed of birds from England, Scotland, Scandinavia, eastern Europe and Iceland. Agricultural and climate changes benefited Starlings and from the mid 19th century they increased as a breeding bird and colonised much of Britain. Starlings need holes and crevices for nesting and pasture for foraging – leatherjackets make up a high proportion of their diet. They nest abundantly in Orkney and can be found in buildings, dykes, cliffs, rabbit burrows and also in heather. There are many post boxes in Orkney that are barred to Starlings! They are great imitators and Orkney's Starling songsters often include the calls of Curlew and Golden Plover. Males and females can be separated – the male's green and purple gloss is stronger and he has a blue base to his bill.

Rosy Starling • Usually with Starlings in summer and autumn; very hard to find

The black and pink adults are unmistakeable; however, the juveniles, which occur in Britain more often than the adults, are buff brown with yellow bills and finding them needs a sharp eye. Feeding on locusts, they are revered on their central Asian breeding grounds as saviours. Easterly winds bring a few birds to Britain in summer and autumn; Orkney's share usually amounts to a couple of birds annually although in 2000 at least six were recorded between June and September from Rendall, Evie, Kirkwall, Westray and North Ronaldsay.

Top: Starlings (male in the foreground) in February at St Nicholas kirk, Holm.

Rosy Starlings (adult left, juvenile on right) in September at the airfield, Sanday.

Jackdaws in April at Nether House, Westray with Langskaill and the Old Manse in the background.

Jackdaw • *Jackie, Kae* • Gardens, towns, cliffs, short grasslands, cereal stubbles and woodlands all year; easy to find

This, the smallest member of the crow family, has a cocky air as it scours pasture for larvae and investigates cowpats. It has beady, pale blue eyes and with its cloak of black and cowl of black and ash-grey, looks ecclesiastical. It is gregarious and breeds colonially in localities that include trees, cliffs, quarries and town centres and although it prefers holes and cavities, occasionally domed nests of stick are built. Jackdaws are plentiful in areas of human habitation that have adjacent good grazing pasture. They nest throughout Britain but are local and thinly distributed in the far north, although they have increased their range in Scotland in the 20th century and even briefly colonised Shetland. In 19th century Orkney they nested in the chimneys of the Earl's Palace in Kirkwall and in the 20th century, small colonies could be found on many of the high cliffs throughout the isles and also with nesting Rooks in Kirkwall, Stromness and Woodwick. Of late the Orkney Jackdaw population has declined and nowadays, although many of these cliff sites are still frequented, numbers have dwindled. In October and November Orkney's resident Jackdaw flocks are supplemented by arrivals from the Continent. The Scandinavian or Nordic birds have grey collars, which grade into white especially on the side of the neck.

Rooks in July on St Magnus Cathedral, Kirkwall – (l-r) Bishop's Palace, Palace Road and Palace Gardens.

Rook • *Corbie* • Gardens, towns, short grasslands, cereal stubbles and woodlands all year; very easy to find

In Orkney, the Rook is a relative newcomer having first nested at Muddiesdale in 1876. Since then, it spread throughout the Mainland and even to South Ronaldsay, Hoy and Rousay. Nowadays the biggest colonies occur in Kirkwall, Stromness and Firth and by the end of the 20th century numbered almost 2,000 nests. Ringing seems to show that breeding birds move freely between Orkney's principal rookeries. In Britain, although absent in most of the uplands, they are widespread in all types of agricultural country as long as small groups of trees are present. Rooks nest early, well before there are leaves on the trees, and the day-to-day life of the rookery is easily observed and is one of wildlife's underrated spectacles. Scotland's rookeries are larger than others, exemplified by Hatton in Aberdeenshire, which in 1957 held 6,700 nests. In winter, roosts draw birds in from further afield; there were 65,000 at one roost in northeast Scotland. Though similar to the Carrion Crow, the Rook can be identified by bare skin around the pale bill and its baggy shorts and looser plumage.

Hooded Crow • *Craa, Hoodie, Grey-back* • Everywhere in town, coast and country all year; very easy to find

In Europe, Hooded Crows occur in northern, central and southern Europe; in Britain, they occur in Ireland and in Scotland north of a line between Glasgow and Aberdeen. They are common birds throughout Orkney and nest on cliffs and electricity poles, in quarries, trees and bushes and on the ground. Flocks of non-breeding birds occur in the West Mainland and sometimes include as many as 100 birds. With their bold pied plumage of black and grey, they are unmistakeable and in Scotland are found in all types of open country including moorland, open woodland, coasts, parks and even city squares. Their long history of persecution stems firstly from the belief that they were symbols of evil portent and secondly from their methodical and relentless pursuit of prey that may include weak and sickly livestock. In fact, they seem capable of eating just about anything from grain, birds' eggs and insects to carrion found at rubbish tips or as road kills.

Carrion Crow • With Hooded Crows all year; hard to find

In areas of Europe without Hooded Crows, it is the Carrion Crow that is in the ascendancy and as the Hoodie retreats in Britain, the Carrion advances. In Orkney, one or two pairs breed annually and it is becoming an increasingly frequent visitor. Dark-billed "Rooks" that lack baggy trousers and that are either solitary or with Hooded Crows are likely to be Carrion Crows.

Hooded Crow (right) and Carrion Crow (left) in autumn at Scapa beach, St Ola.

Raven • *Corbie, Ramna, Hrafn* • Everywhere all year especially coasts and uplands; very easy to find

With its far-carrying "*pruuk*" call, tumbling acrobatic flights and characteristic wedge-shaped tail, the Raven is a familiar sight in Orkney's skies. There are at least 100 pairs throughout the islands; a handful nest in trees, on inland crags or quarries but the vast majority choose sea cliffs. Their commonness has not always been the case; up until the end of the 19th century, when persecution was at its peak, there were probably no more than ten pairs including a pair that nested on St Magnus Cathedral. A similar picture is painted for Britain; once so widespread they could be found scavenging the streets of London, by the start of the 20th century they had retreated to remote coastal and upland areas in the west and north. They are early nesters; eggs are frequently laid before the beginning of March resulting in April chicks. As a species, Ravens are fairly sedentary but research has demonstrated that the county's young Ravens travel widely among the islands and even venture further south into the Scottish Highlands to nest. During an Orkney winter, plentiful supplies of carrion can attract gatherings of more than 100 birds.

Raven and nest during April at Sacquoy Head, Rousay with Westray in the background.

191

*House Sparrows (male left, female right) in May near Hellia Gibb, Sandwick –
(l-r), Skaill House, Skara Brae and Skaill farm.*

House Sparrow • *Sprog* • Gardens, towns and farms all year;
very easy to find

For many years in Britain, the House Sparrow was considered
to be a serious agricultural pest; indeed its impact upon crops
was deemed to be so great that sparrow clubs, whose aim was
to destroy as many of these birds as possible, flourished during
the 19th century. From this position of being a very abundant
bird, the House Sparrow has undergone an alarming decline. It
is reckoned that between the years 1994 and 2000, London lost
three quarters of its birds. The main cause of its decline appears
to be due to a decrease in insects that House Sparrow chicks are
dependent on and it's probable that crop spraying and garden
pesticides have contributed to this decline. However, it is still a
widespread bird in Britain and can be found almost everywhere in
coexistence with man and his animal associates. In Orkney it was
described as "abounding in myriads" in the 18th century and even
though it is still abundant and found countywide, there has been a
very noticeable falling off of numbers. Although in southern Britain
House Sparrows frequently build nests in hedgerows, elsewhere
they are predominantly hole nesters choosing buildings, dykes and
even nest boxes specifically earmarked for Blue Tits and House
Martins. The males have grey crowns and black bibs while the
grey and buff colours of the female are noticeably nondescript.

Chaffinches (female left, male right) in May at Happy Valley, Stenness.

Chaffinch • Gardens, woodlands, set-aside and cereal stubbles all year; easy to find

This is a widespread and abundant bird and its sharp metallic "*pink*" call and rolling, rattling song are some of the most familiar sounds in Britain. One reason for its abundance is its catholic tastes; unlike some other finches it does not have a specialised bill and therefore is able to consume a varied diet. The densest populations are found in mature broad-leaved woodland but Chaffinches are likely to be found wherever there are trees and bushes. In Europe over the last 100 years they have spread northwards and this is reflected in Britain by the colonisation of some Hebridean islands. Additionally, there has also been an increase of breeding birds in Orkney and nowadays pairs can be found in the woodlands of Hoy, the Mainland, Rousay and Shapinsay. In the main British Chaffinches are sedentary birds but in winter birds from Scandinavia arrive to augment the resident population; ringing has illustrated that some of Orkney's winter Chaffinches are Norwegian by birth. Many of these migrants are females; the solo males remain on territory in Scandinavia giving rise to its alternative name "*bachelor bird*". The plumage of the sexes is quite different; the male has a blue-grey crown and orange-pink breast while the female is essentially green-brown and buff. Both have dazzling white wing bars.

Tree Sparrow • Coasts, farms and set aside, possibly with House Sparrows; very hard to find

As with the House Sparrow, a massive population decline has been experienced by its close relative the Tree Sparrow. It is estimated that there has been a 95% reduction since 1975. Changes in farming practices, most especially the increase of autumn sown crops, have resulted in a much-reduced supply of weed seeds and spilt grain. Over much of lowland England, Wales and Scotland, Tree Sparrows occur in open woodland and hedgerows on farmland or at the edge of built up areas. It is largely sedentary but is also noted for inexplicable irruptive movements that have led to the intermittent colonisation of fringe areas. The Faeroe Islands have been colonised briefly on three occasions in the past 100 years, the last instance occurring in 1960. It is highly likely that this particular irrruptive movement is linked to the colonisation by up to 12 pairs of the coniferous woodland at Carrick House on Eday between 1961 and 1974. Prior to this nests were reported in 1882 and 1916 at Berstane and Binscarth respectively. More recently a pair were in residence on Papay in 1972 and a single bird hybridised with House Sparrows on North Ronaldsay during the 1990s. Migrating birds are not common but most sightings have occurred in May. The sexes are similar and with a chestnut crown and black spot in the middle of its white cheek, the Tree Sparrow's plumage gives a crisp, smart and dapper impression.

Tree Sparrows in April at Carrick plantation, Eday – (l-r) Calf of Eday, Calf Sound, Carrick House and Sanday.

Brambling • Gardens, set-aside and cereal stubbles in autumn, winter and spring; not easy to find

This, the northern counterpart to the Chaffinch, is essentially a winter visitor to Britain. Beechmast is the preferred food and the Brambling's winter distribution is determined by the availability of this crop; consequently birds wander widely over Europe each year and rarely spend successive winters at the same locality. If beechmast is unavailable other food sources are exploited and Bramblings can be found at sewage farms, gardens, open fields, set-aside and shoreline. As a breeding bird, the Brambling has the merest of toeholds in Britain and first bred on Hoy in 1988. In most years one or two pairs attempt to nest in Britain; however in 1998 there were at least eight pairs in Scotland. The winter plumage of both sexes is similar – a combination of black, brown and orange. The white rump is a give away characteristic. Scandinavian born birds pass through Orkney during late September and October some journeying as far as Belgium before reappearing in March and April on their northbound schedule.

Bramblings (male left, female right) in November at Echna, Burray –
(l-r) Echnaloch Bay, A961, Echna Loch.

Greenfinch • Gardens, woodlands, set-aside and cereal stubbles all year; easy to find

Historically, Greenfinches were birds of the forest edge and in some parts of Europe they still are. In Britain they are typical garden birds and now thrive in mature ornamental gardens, churchyards and parks where they tend to breed in loose colonies. They have always been associated with human habitation especially farmland, villages and towns but of late have become less abundant on farmland. Weed seeds and spilt grain are now less available due to pesticides and changes in farming practices and Greenfinches have taken very readily to feeding at bird tables. They are absent from treeless areas but more planting of woodland has resulted in an expansion of their range in the 20th century. It was in 1880 that the county's first breeding pair was noted at Swanbister in Orphir and during much of the 20th century the species was considered to be fairly common and could be found in small numbers on the Mainland, Hoy, Shapinsay and Rousay. However during the early 1970s, Orkney's Greenfinches vanished for almost five years only to recolonise strongly as a result of an influx in 1976. At present breeding birds can be found in their previous sites and also on Burray, Eday and South Ronaldsay. Winter flocks of Greenfinches have become commonplace and may hold as many as 250 birds. Studies through ringing have shown that these winter flocks frequently include birds of Continental, particularly Norwegian, origin. Both the male and the female are yellow green with vivid yellow markings on the wing; the male however is brighter and in pristine conjugal plumage, quite exotic. Their liquid song, nasal wheeze and butterfly display flight in spring means that they are fairly easy to locate.

Left: Greenfinches (female left, male right) in May on the Hill of Midland, Orphir – (l-r) Houton Pier, Bay of Houton, Midland Ness, Cava and the Holm of Houton.

Above: Siskins (male left, female right) in May at Queenamidda, Rendall – background, Hackland Hill and Enyas Hill.

Siskin • Gardens, set-aside and cereal stubbles in spring and autumn; hard to find

These tiny finches are primarily associated with conifers and in the 19th century breeding birds were confined to Scotland's Caledonian pine forests. However, with increased planting and maturing of conifers Siskins can now be found in much of Scotland, Wales and northern England. Their success has also been aided by the recent trend to visit gardens in winter. Along with Redpolls, Siskins are the smallest finches that are likely to be seen in Orkney. The greens and yellows in their plumage are similar to Greenfinch colours, but unlike Greenfinches, both male and female Siskins are streaked with black and the male has a bold black bib, face and crown. They are usually seen in gardens during autumn, winter and spring and are agile and acrobatic visitors to peanut and seed feeders. Siskins are irruptive birds and in autumn a poor crop of spruce and pine seeds in Scandinavia may be the reason for large numbers to pass overhead or indeed linger in Orkney. In recent years, conifer stands on Hoy and in Rendall have been homes to nesting birds.

Goldfinch • Gardens, set-aside and cereal stubbles in autumn, winter and spring; hard to find

In the last few years, Goldfinches have become much more frequent in Orkney. From being a rare visitor it is now seen in the county annually and on occasion small flocks can be found in set-aside crops during the autumn and winter months. There is even a strong possibility that Goldfinches may soon breed in Orkney following the appearance of singing birds in successive years during springtime in Finstown. Their increase in the county is in line with their general spread throughout Britain. At the end of the 19th century, Goldfinches were nearly extinct due to the bird's popularity as a cage bird. However following campaigns from the Society for the Protection of Birds, trapping was banned in 1881. The birds prospered and colonised a variety of habitats; their main requirement was an abundant supply of seeds from plants such as thistle, teasel, burdock and knapweed. Goldfinches are absent from upland areas and in Britain are most abundant south of a line between the Humber and the Dee. However, in the last fifty years their range in Scotland has expanded especially in the northeast with a thriving core population around the Moray Firth. The majority of Britain's birds spend the winter in Belgium, France or Spain. Their unmistakeable plumage accounts for local names such as *"the tailor of London"* and with their soft tinkling calls it is little wonder that collectively, Goldfinches are referred to as a charm.

Goldfinch in March above Stenaday, Heddle Road, Finstown, Firth – (l-r) Scarva Taing, Bay of Firth, Damsay and Holm of Grimbister with Wide Firth beyond.

Crossbill • Coasts, woodlands and uplands in summer and autumn; hard to find

With their large heads, colourful plumage, bill shape and sidling gait, Crossbills have more than a passing resemblance to parrots. The adult males are red, the females greeny-yellow and the youngsters streaky brown. Coniferous areas throughout Britain are homes in both summer and winter to Crossbills; their strongholds are in the Scottish Highlands, Northumberland, Wales, East Anglia and the New Forest. These populations are supplemented in some years by large numbers that invade Britain from Europe and further east in search of their principal food, the seeds of spruces and pines. It is in irruption years that they are most frequently seen in Orkney when they can be found as early as June and July in plantations, gardens, on the hill or at the coast. One of the first indications of their presence is their metallic "*jip, jip*" call and flocks can be quite approachable.

Linnet • *Lintie, Rose Lintie, Lintick* • Rural gardens, set-aside and cereal stubbles all year; easy to find

During Victorian times, the Linnet was much sought after as a cage bird. With red foreheads and breasts and cinnamon backs, cock Linnets are attractive. Coupled with a song considered to be the most beautiful of any finch, its popularity as a captive bird was such that its numbers in Britain were at a low ebb before protective

Crossbills (male on left, female on right) in August at the Glen, Rackwick, Hoy with Broadiface in the background.

Linnets (female on left, male on right) in May at Samsonslane, Stronsay.

Right: Lesser Redpoll (left) and Common Redpoll (right) in spring at the Deerness slip, Deerness with Newark Bay in the background.

legislation was introduced at the end of the 19th century. It is principally a bird of the lowlands where it nests in open country and is invariably associated with gorse bushes, a link which has given rise to colourful vernacular names such as *"gorse thatcher"* in Shropshire, *"furze linnet"* in Northamptonshire and *"whin grey"* in Northern Ireland. Unfortunately their recovery has been short-lived and the British population is generally in decline. Linnets appear to be more dependent on weed seeds than any other finch and the increased use of herbicides has affected their chief food supply. As well as a scarcity of arable weeds in modern times, the Linnet's struggle has been compounded by afforestation, the removal of hedgerows and improvements to rough grazing. Of late they have gravitated more to gardens where nesting sites are assured and food supplies are more constant. Scotland's nesting Linnets predominate in farmed areas of the lowlands and the east coast and are absent from the Highlands, the Hebrides, much of the north and west coast and Shetland. In Orkney breeding birds were deemed to be common in the 19th century and could be found on most of the islands and they are still widely distributed around the county especially where there are bushes. Study has indicated that many of Orkney's summer Linnets spend the winter in the Moray Firth area. During the winter, Linnet numbers dwindle but small flocks may be found feeding on set-aside, cereal stubbles, mudflats and saltmarshes. Again, through ringing research, it has been discovered that the flocks include Continental-born birds.

Lesser Redpoll • Coasts, set-aside and cereal stubbles in autumn, winter and spring; hard to find

The smallest of the redpoll family is the brownish-buff Lesser Redpoll that can be found breeding in Britain, Ireland, the Alps and coastal northwest Europe. With its straw-coloured bill, red patch on its forehead and a small back bib, the Lesser Redpoll is a smart trapeze artist feeding acrobatically in the branches of trees such as silver birch and alder. In the last fifty years they have benefited from the increased planting of upland moors and lowland heaths and can now be found over much of Britain, even becoming loosely established in peripheral areas such as Cornwall, Pembrokeshire, Caithness and the Outer Hebrides. Such has been its success that some of the British population has colonised newly afforested dunes in the Netherlands. Even Orkney has experienced a few instances of nesting; pairs have been located in Rendall, Deerness and on Hoy in recent years. It is much better known as an autumn and winter visitor.

Common Redpoll • Coasts, set-aside and cereal stubbles in autumn, winter and spring; hard to find

No less arboreally acrobatic is the slightly larger, paler and greyer Common Redpoll that hails from the birch forests and pinewoods of Scandinavia. As with some other seed-eating species from this part of the world, food shortages trigger irruptions that deposit migrating birds on Britain's and Orkney's eastern shores especially during October and November. It's probable that following one of these irruptions a pair in 1976 remained to breed in the White Glen plantation on Hoy.

Twite • *Heather Lintie* • Maritime heath, moorlands, set-aside and cereal stubbles all year; easy to find

This little brown finch has a very intriguing ancestry. It seems originally to have spread from Tibet into central Europe then, as the ice edge retreated into northern and western Europe, some birds followed while others returned to Asia. Consequently the species has two centres of population some 2500 kilometres apart. Twites are birds of open treeless country; breeding birds favour heather moors and coastal cliff edges while wintering birds can be found in set-aside, cereal stubbles, salt marshes, coastal fields and on the tide line. They tend to be found in harsher and higher environments than Linnets and in Britain are most abundant in north and west Scotland, Ireland and the south Pennines. Like all other finches they have experienced recent declines due to the increased use of herbicides and the resulting lack of weed seeds and also the loss of moorland habitats due to reclamation for agriculture or forestry. Orkney has witnessed a similar decline and although it is widely distributed and probably breeds on most islands, the Twite is not numerous. Winter flocks can hold up to 500 birds and ringing has demonstrated that some of these visiting birds originate from Shetland, northern Scotland and Scandinavia. Twites appear darker streaked than Linnets. In winter when confusion is most likely, look out for the Twite's orange-buff throats and yellow bills. They also show less white than Linnets in both tail and wings. The calls can be similar but the Twite has a very nasal and whiney "*twite*" call.

Rosefinch • Coasts, scrub and woodlands in spring and autumn; very hard to find

The male has a head, throat and rump of vibrant scarlet that gave rise to a former name *"Scarlet Rosefinch"*. Occasionally birds in this spring finery are seen in the county and even heard in song. Mostly however, Rosefinches occur in the autumn and refer to birds out of their bright breeding plumage; females and young individuals appear anything but inspiring. Indeed, adjectives such as "bland", "featureless" and "nondescript" are frequently used to describe the bird in the guise in which it is most frequently seen in. Consequently Rosefinches must be overlooked on a frequent basis. It is sparrow-sized, thick-necked and thickset with a dark beady eye peering from its pale featureless face and two thin white wing bars. It is, however, a very successful species and has expanded its world range more than any other bird except the Collared Dove. Until 1900, it had nested no further west than Russia; since then it has colonised much of Scandinavia and has bred occasionally in Scotland. It chooses a wide variety of habitats to nest in including scrub, swamp and gardens.

Left: Twites in winter at Rosebank, Burray – (l-r) Water Sound, Knockhall point, St Margaret's Hope and M.V.Claymore.

Rosefinch (male) in May above Feold, Lyde Road, Rendall – (l-r) Enyas Hill, Gorseness and Bay of Isbister.

Hawfinch (male) in April at Nearhouse, Sanday.

Hawfinch • Coasts, gardens and woodlands in spring and autumn; very hard to find

These are the biggest of the finches likely to be seen in Orkney and though never as numerous as Bullfinches and Crossbills, are recorded annually in small numbers from gardens countywide. It's very likely that the majority of the birds have been blown eastwards from the Continent where they breed no further north than southern Sweden and Finland. They are shy and secretive birds of deciduous woodland, needing a mixture of trees such as beech, hornbeam, wych elm, wild cherry and maple. In Britain, their stronghold is in the southeast of England with local pockets in the Midlands and the North. Scotland's share is limited to a few sites in Perthshire and the Lothians. They are heavy-looking birds, colourfully marked and show a broad white wing bar in flight and at rest. The females are duller than the males. However, despite their splendid looks, their shyness means that they are able to go undetected. A loud and explosive "*tic*" call may be the first indication of its presence.

Bullfinches (female left, male right) in December at Burnside, Stromness.

Bullfinch • Gardens and scrub in autumn and winter; hard to find

In some years, autumn and winter in Orkney is enlivened by the presence of Scandinavian Bullfinches that have crossed the North Sea in search of food and clement weather. On arrival they are most likely to be found near eastern coasts but quickly find their way to town and country gardens where they feed on seeds and berries. With a splendid combination of colours, they are handsome and easy to recognise; both sexes have black caps, white rumps and a white wing bar but the male has a salmon pink breast and grey back, while the female is buff-pink. Their normal call is a soft whistle but in 2004 strange trumpet-like calls were heard in Orkney, an indication that these particular birds were of a population that had journeyed from Russia and Siberia. Throughout the rest of Britain Bullfinches are widespread and it is only in treeless areas such as the Highlands and Islands that they are absent. They are resident and sedentary wherever there is an ample supply of weed and tree seeds and tangled bushes for nesting. In some parts of Britain they are pests to commercial orchards and fruit growers because of their liking for the flower heads of fruit trees. Their notoriety for damage was recognised as long ago as Elizabethan times when a bounty of a penny a head was offered by the state.

Yellowhammer • *Yellow Yarling* • Cereal stubbles in autumn and winter; very hard to find

Across Britain it is a breeding bird of open country invariably associated with gorse. Its song, perennially translated as "*a little bit of bread and no cheese*", cascades over heaths, commons, woodland edges, hedgerows and railway embankments. Although found over most of the United Kingdom, like other country birds it has experienced recent declines due to the removal of hedges and increased use of herbicides. Depressingly it has been lost from Orkney as a nesting bird; the last pair was in Orphir in 1975. During the 19th century, they were considered to be more common than the Corn Bunting around Kirkwall and Finstown and resident on Hoy, Rousay and Shapinsay. On the South Isles, encouraged by the sowing of whin hedges, they were abundant. However by 1960, Yellowhammers had become very scarce in all their former strongholds. Nowadays, apart from occasional birds probably of Scandinavian origin seen on spring and autumn passage, the most likely place to encounter Yellowhammers is during winter at set-aside crops. There remain ample tracts of suitable gorse habitat within the county and the return of the "*Yarling*" as a nesting bird may yet occur. The male is yellower than the female; both sexes have rusty-red rumps.

Yellowhammers (female left, male right) in spring at Holodyke, Harray – background, the Loch of Harray, Ward Hill and the Cuilags, Hoy.

Lapland Bunting • Coasts, set-aside and cereal stubbles in autumn; very hard to find

This is one of the commonest nesting birds in the arctic tundra; it even bred in Scotland during the 1970s with up to 11 pairs in the far north. There are two widely separated populations: the Greenland birds which usually spend the winter in North America and the Scandinavian birds that usually migrate southeast into Asia. Britain's wintering population usually amounts to no more than 500 birds and it's considered that birds from both populations are involved. During their stay, the "*longspurs*", as they are known in North America, associate with Skylarks, finches and other buntings. They feed in stubble and on rough grassland in coastal fields on England's east coast between Northumberland and Kent. In Orkney, the most likely place to see Lapland Buntings is on North Ronaldsay where they occur sparingly on passage in spring and more frequently in autumn. The birds are great runners and scurry furtively through low vegetation. With black face and chest and white zigzag, the spring male is very recognisable; in autumn, females and immatures look open-faced and have chestnut napes and wing panels. Listen for the definitive "*ticky ticky teu*" call.

Lapland Buntings (female on left, male on right) in October at New Mill, Nesstoun – background, Linklet Bay and Ness Toun.

207

Snow Bunting • *Oatfowl, Snowbird, Snowflake* • Uplands, cereal stubbles and soft coasts in autumn, winter and spring; easy to find

Flocks of Snow Buntings spill into Britain towards the end of September from their summer homes in Greenland, Iceland and northern Europe to spend the winter along the east coast or in upland areas. Typically the birds choose areas of short open vegetation, preferring to pick seeds from the ground or from low-growing plants. Sand dunes are favoured sites and each year in Orkney flocks are recorded from sandy areas such as the Birsay links, Scapa beach, Bu sands and No 4 barrier. Flocks also gravitate to stubble fields especially those with standing water for drinking and bathing. It is also possible to see Snow Buntings in Orkney's hill country during winter where they are likely to be the only small bird encountered. Listen out for their rippling, rolling calls. Flocks in Orkney seem to be decreasing in size and the four figure counts of fifty years ago (both Balfour and Groundwater refer to flocks of 5,000 birds) are a fading memory. Groundwater also makes reference to the practice of catching Snow Buntings in the stackyards and it is apparent that the birds were welcome additions to the Orkney winter diet. Snow Buntings are breeding birds of the high Arctic and nest farther north than any other passerine – there are instances of nesting north of 80°. Sometimes referred to as the *"Inuit Sparrow"*, not only can they be found on tundra and mountain tops, but also in Spitsbergen and Greenland, dwelling in towns. There is even a breeding population in highland Scotland with up to 100 pairs nesting in the summer snowfields – their nests can be lined with the fur of

Snow Buntings in January at the Broch of Gurness, Evie – background, Eynhallow Sound and Blotchnie Fiold, Rousay.

Red Deer and Mountain Hare and the feathers of Golden Eagle, Ptarmigan and Dotterel. The male's body and wings show a great deal of white, while the females and youngsters have more brown and russet in their plumage. Birds in their spectacular black and white summer dress are less often seen in Orkney but can be encountered in April and May.

Corn Bunting • *Skitterbroltie, Common Bunting, Thistle-cock* • Farm yards, cereal fields, set-aside and cereal stubbles all year; very hard to find

It is difficult to believe how numerous Corn Buntings once were in Orkney. Their distinctive and unmusical jingling song was a feature of all the cultivated isles. Low refers to them as being "shot in farm yards in winter in great numbers; it is good eating being full and fat"; it appears they were an integral element of the Orkney diet in the 18th and 19th centuries. Towards the end of the 19th century it was regarded as a common resident on all the cultivated isles – in 1892 there were considered to be 16 pairs on North Ronaldsay. In the 20th century there was a rapid decline throughout Britain and northwest Europe; a host of reasons have been cited including the mechanisation of harvesting, increased use of herbicides, the disappearance of traditional rotations and the overall reduction of winter seed supplies. Orkney has mirrored the British and European decline; by 1940 they were thinly scattered across the Mainland leaving the north isles, principally Sanday and Stronsay, with the county's core population. However by the end of the century they were no longer resident in Orkney; the last nesting pair was on Stronsay in 1993. No Corn Buntings have been seen in the county since the spring of 1999 when a bird was present at Dale, Stronsay. In Britain, the Corn Bunting's remaining strongholds are the arable farmlands of eastern England and northeast Scotland.

Reed Bunting • Wetlands with scrub, set-aside and cereal stubbles all year; easy to find

Well within living memory, three species of bunting (Yellowhammer, Corn and Reed Bunting) could be found nesting within the county. Nowadays the sole survivor is the Reed Bunting whose fortunes have waxed and waned since the beginning of the 19th century when it was considered to be uncommon. Even in 1925, it was regarded as the scarcest of the three but by the 1940s had increased significantly. This expansion was in line with the national trend that witnessed the colonisation of Shetland in 1949. Throughout Britain lowland wetland habitats are primarily chosen for nesting but the Reed Bunting's spread

Corn Bunting in March near the Moncur Memorial Church, Stronsay.

has been aided by a willingness to breed in drier locations such as hedgerows, marginal land and even conifer plantations. They have also become frequent visitors to bird tables. Typically it can be found perched on top of reeds or rushes uttering its thin song (which has been described as being among the least noteworthy of any of our songbirds) or "*tsoo*" call. In Orkney it is still fairly easy to locate in the appropriate breeding habitat and can be found on most islands, but a decrease has been obvious recently (since 1998 the annual Orkney bird report has described the Reed Bunting as a declining resident breeding species). Drained wetlands and the increased use of herbicides have affected the Reed Bunting's breeding opportunities and its livelihood after the breeding season has been influenced by a reduction in available food due to changes in agricultural practices. During the winter flocks gather to exploit set-aside and cereal stubbles and it is likely that Scandinavian birds arrive to supplement the Orkney populations; one particular set-aside scheme, Dale in Evie, annually sustains flocks of up to 200 birds. With their black heads, white collars and moustaches, the males are unmistakeable; the females are less obvious but usually show a buff supercilium and a pale moustache. Both sexes show white outer-tail feathers as they fly away.

Reed Buntings (female left, male right) in March at Voy mill, Stromness.

211

The full Orkney list

Correct to 31st July, 2011. Updated by Paul Higson

The total of different bird species seen in Britain stands at 579 and a handful of well-travelled birdwatchers have seen over 500 of these. Up until the end of 1997, the number of species recorded in Orkney was 390 and a few of Orkney's dedicated birders have reached the 300 mark. The Orkney Book of Birds contains I87 species and these are marked in **bold** in the following table that lists all the species that have been recorded in the county. The occurrences relate to all records in the 20th and 21st century except where specifically noted.

Category A consists of species that have been recorded in an apparently natural state at least once since 1 January, 1950 (except where stated).

Category D consists of species that would otherwise appear in the main list (Category A) except that there is reasonable doubt that they have ever occurred in a natural state.

Category E consists of species that have been recorded as introductions, transportees or escapees from captivity.

No	Species	Scientific Name	occurrences
	Category A		
1	**Mute Swan**	*Cygnus olor*	
2	**Bewick's Swan**	*Cygnus columbianus*	22
3	**Whooper Swan**	*Cygnus cygnus*	
4	Bean Goose	*Anser fabalis*	
5	**Pink-footed Goose**	*Anser brachyrhynchus*	
6	**White-fronted Goose**	*Anser albifrons*	
7	**Greylag Goose**	*Anser anser*	
8	Snow Goose	*Anser caerulescens*	30
9	Canada Goose	*Branta canadensis*	
10	**Barnacle Goose**	*Branta leucopsis*	
11	**Brent Goose**	*Branta bernicla*	
12	Ruddy Shelduck	*Tadorna ferruginea*	5
13	**Shelduck**	*Tadorna tadorna*	
14	Mandarin Duck	*Aix galericulata*	12
15	**Wigeon**	*Anas penelope*	

	Annual number of breeding pairs	**Annual number of non-breeding individuals**
Very rare	Up to 10 breeding records in total	Up to 10 records in total
Rare	1 – 10	1 – 10
Uncommon	11 – 100	11 – 100
Fairly common	101 – 1,000	101 – 1,000
Common	1,001 – 10,000	1,001 – 10,000
Abundant	10,000 +	10,000 +

Last accepted record	
	Fairly common resident breeding species
2010	Rare
	Fairly common on passage and in winter
	Rare
	Fairly common on passage and in winter
	Fairly common but localised in winter
	Fairly common breeding species, abundant on passage and in winter
2011	Rare, but first bred in 2009
	Rare
	Common on passage and in winter
	Uncommon
2000	Very rare
	Fairly common breeding species, rare in early winter
2010	Very rare
	Uncommon breeding species, common on passage and in winter

No	Species	Scientific Name	occur.
16	American Wigeon	*Anas americana*	32
17	**Gadwall**	*Anas strepera*	
18	**Teal**	*Anas crecca*	
19	Green-winged Teal	*Anas carolinensis*	31
20	**Mallard**	*Anas platyrhynchos*	
21	**Pintail**	*Anas acuta*	
22	**Garganey**	*Anas querquedula*	
23	Blue-winged Teal	*Anas discors*	12
24	**Shoveler**	*Anas clypeata*	
25	Red Crested Pochard	*Netta rufina*	5
26	Canvasback	*Aythya valisineria*	2
27	**Pochard**	*Aythya ferina*	
28	Ring-necked Duck	*Aythya collaris*	7
29	Ferruginous Duck	*Aythya nyroca*	1
30	**Tufted Duck**	*Aythya fuligula*	
31	**Scaup**	*Aythya marila*	
32	Lesser Scaup	*Aythya affinis*	3
33	**Eider**	*Somateria mollissima*	
34	King Eider	*Somateria spectabilis*	24
35	Steller's Eider	*Polysticta stelleri*	5
36	**Long-tailed Duck**	*Clangula hyemalis*	
37	**Common Scoter**	*Melanitta nigra*	
38	Surf Scoter	*Melanitta perspicillata*	
39	**Velvet Scoter**	*Melanitta fusca*	
40	**Goldeneye**	*Bucephala clangula*	
41	**Smew**	*Mergellus albellus*	
42	**Red-breasted Merganser**	*Mergus serrator*	
43	**Goosander**	*Mergus merganser*	
44	**Ruddy Duck**	*Oxyura jamaicensis*	
45	**Red Grouse**	*Lagopus lagopus*	
46	Ptarmigan	*Lagopus muta*	
47	Black Grouse	*Tetrao tetrix*	
48	**Red-legged Partridge**	*Alectoris rufa*	
49	**Grey Partridge**	*Perdix perdix*	
50	Quail	*Coturnix coturnix*	
51	**Pheasant**	*Phasianus colchicus*	
52	**Red-throated Diver**	*Gavia stellata*	

Last ac. record	
2010	Rare
	Rare breeding species, uncommon on passage and in winter
	Fairly common breeding species, common on passage and in winter
2011	Rare
	Common breeding, passage and wintering species
	Uncommon breeding and wintering species
	Very rare breeding species and rare summer visitor
2010	Rare
	Uncommon breeding and wintering species
2003	Very rare
2001	Very rare
	Rare breeding species and common in winter
2011	Very rare
1981	Very rare
	Fairly common breeding and wintering species
	Fairly common in winter, has bred
2010	Very rare
	Common breeding and wintering species
2010	Rare
1982	Very rare
	Common in winter, has bred
	Uncommon visitor, has bred
	Rare
	Fairly common in winter
	Fairly common in winter
	Rare in winter
	Fairly common breeding and wintering species
	Rare
	Rare breeding species and uncommon visitor
	Fairly common resident breeding species
	Extinct breeding species, last seen c.1831
	Extinct – introduction in 19th century failed
	Rare breeding species – introduced
	Very rare breeding species – introduced
	Very rare breeding species and rare summer visitor
	Fairly common breeding species – introduced
	Fairly common breeding species, uncommon in winter

No	Species	Scientific Name	occur.
53	**Black-throated Diver**	*Gavia arctica*	
54	**Great Northern Diver**	*Gavia immer*	
55	White-billed Diver	*Gavia adamsii*	41
56	**Little Grebe**	*Tachybaptus ruficollis*	
57	Great Crested Grebe	*Podiceps cristatus*	
58	**Red-necked Grebe**	*Podiceps grisegena*	
59	**Slavonian Grebe**	*Podiceps auritus*	
60	Black-necked Grebe	*Podiceps nigricollis*	3
61	Black-browed Albatross	*Thalassarche melanophris*	2
62	**Fulmar**	*Fulmarus glacialis*	
63	Fea's/Zino's Petrel	*Pterodroma feae/madeira*	2
64	Cory's Shearwater	*Calonectris diomedea*	21
65	Great Shearwater	*Puffinus gravis*	
66	**Sooty Shearwater**	*Puffinus griseus*	
67	**Manx Shearwater**	*Puffinus puffinus*	
68	Balearic Shearwater	*Puffinus mauretanicus*	15
69	**Storm Petrel**	*Hydrobates pelagicus*	
70	**Leach's Petrel**	*Oceanodroma leucorhoa*	
71	**Gannet**	*Morus bassanus*	
72	**Cormorant**	*Phalacrocorax carbo*	
73	**Shag**	*Phalacrocorax aristotelis*	
74	Bittern	*Botaurus stellaris*	7
75	Little Bittern	*Ixobrychus minutus*	2
76	Night Heron	*Nycticorax nycticorax*	6
77	Squacco Heron	*Ardeola ralloides*	1
78	Little Egret	*Egretta garzetta*	17
79	Great White Egret	*Ardea alba*	6
80	**Grey Heron**	*Ardea cinerea*	
81	Purple Heron	*Ardea purpurea*	2
82	Black Stork	*Ciconia nigra*	5
83	White Stork	*Ciconia ciconia*	6
84	Glossy Ibis	*Plegadis falcinellus*	4
85	Spoonbill	*Platalea leucorodia*	5
86	Honey Buzzard	*Pernis apivorus*	
87	Black Kite	*Milvus migrans*	8
88	Red Kite	*Milvus milvus*	17
89	**White-tailed Eagle**	*Haliaeetus albicilla*	
90	**Marsh Harrier**	*Circus aeruginosus*	

Last ac. record	
	Uncommon on passage and in winter
	Common in winter
2011	Rare
	Uncommon breeding and wintering species
	Rare
	Uncommon on passage and in winter
	Fairly common on passage and in winter
2004	Very rare
1975	Very rare
	Abundant resident breeding species
2010	Very rare
2009	Rare
	Rare
	Common on passage especially in autumn
	Uncommon breeding species and fairly common on passage
2010	Rare
	Common breeding and passage species
	Very rare breeding and passage species
	Common breeding and passage species
	Fairly common breeding and wintering species
	Common breeding and wintering species
2010	Very rare
1971	Very rare
1998	Very rare
1896	Very rare
2010	Rare
2009	Very rare
	Very rare breeding species, fairly common on passage and in winter
1982	Very rare
2008	Very rare
2008	Very rare
2000	Very rare
1998	Very rare
	Rare
2011	Very rare
2011	Very rare
	Rare, has bred
	Very rare breeding species and uncommon on passage

No	Species	Scientific Name	occur.
91	**Hen Harrier**	Circus cyaneus	
92	Pallid Harrier	Circus macrourus	1
93	Montagu's Harrier	Circus pygargus	1
94	Goshawk	Accipiter gentilis	34
95	**Sparrowhawk**	Accipiter nisus	
96	**Common Buzzard**	Buteo buteo	
97	Rough-legged Buzzard	Buteo lagopus	
98	**Golden Eagle**	Aquila chrysaetos	
99	**Osprey**	Pandion haliaetus	
100	**Kestrel**	Falco tinnunculus	
101	Red-footed Falcon	Falco vespertinus	16
102	**Merlin**	Falco columbarius	
103	Hobby	Falco subbuteo	
104	Gyr Falcon	Falco rusticolus	22
105	**Peregrine Falcon**	Falco peregrinus	
106	**Water Rail**	Rallus aquaticus	
107	**Spotted Crake**	Porzana porzana	
108	**Corncrake**	Crex crex	
109	**Moorhen**	Gallinula chloropus	
110	**Coot**	Fulica atra	
111	Crane	Grus grus	
112	Little Bustard	Tetrax tetrax	1
113	Great Bustard	Otis tarda	1
114	Sandhill Crane	Grus canadensis	1
115	**Oystercatcher**	Haematopus ostralegus	
116	Black-winged Stilt	Himantopus himantopus	1
117	Avocet	Recurvirostra avosetta	13
118	Stone Curlew	Burhinus oedicnemus	2
119	Collared Pratincole	Glareola pratincola	2
120	Little Ringed Plover	Charadrius dubius	7
121	**Ringed Plover**	Charadrius hiaticula	
122	Greater Sand Plover	Charadrius leschenaultii	1
123	Dotterel	Charadrius morinellus	
124	American Golden Plover	Pluvialis dominica	25
125	Pacific Golden Plover	Pluvialis fulva	9
126	**Golden Plover**	Pluvialis apricaria	

Last ac. record	
	Uncommon resident breeding, passage and wintering species
1995	Very rare
1996	Very rare
2011	Rare
	Rare resident breeding species and uncommon on passage
	Rare resident breeding species and uncommon on passage
	Rare on passage and in winter
	Rare, has bred
	Rare
	Uncommon breeding, passage and wintering species
2006	Rare
	Uncommon breeding, passage and wintering species
	Rare
2006	Rare
	Uncommon resident breeding species
	Rare breeding species, uncommon on passage and in winter
	Very rare breeding species and rare visitor
	Uncommon breeding species and passage visitor
	Fairly common breeding, passage and wintering species
	Uncommon breeding species and common in winter
	Rare
1989	Very rare
1924	Very rare
2009	Very rare
	Common breeding species and passage visitor, fairly common in winter
1814	Very rare
2009	Very rare
2010	Very rare
2003	Very rare
2011	Very rare
	Fairly common breeding, passage and wintering species
1979	Very rare
	Rare visitor, has bred
2010	Rare
2011	Very rare
	Uncommon breeding species, common on passage and in winter

No	Species	Scientific Name	occur.
127	**Grey Plover**	*Pluvialis squatarola*	
128	Sociable Plover	*Vanellus gregarius*	3
129	**Lapwing**	*Vanellus vanellus*	
130	**Knot**	*Calidris canutus*	
131	**Sanderling**	*Calidris alba*	
132	Semipalmated Sandpiper	*Calidris pusilla*	3
133	Western Sandpiper	*Calidris mauri*	1
134	Little Stint	*Calidris minuta*	
135	Temminck's Stint	*Calidris temminckii*	14
136	White-rumped Sandpiper	*Calidris fuscicollis*	18
137	Baird's Sandpiper	*Calidris bairdii*	1
138	Pectoral Sandpiper	*Calidris melanotos*	
139	Curlew Sandpiper	*Calidris ferruginea*	
140	**Purple Sandpiper**	*Calidris maritima*	
141	**Dunlin**	*Calidris alpina*	
142	Broad-billed Sandpiper	*Limicola falcinellus*	2
143	Buff-breasted Sandpiper	*Tryngites subruficollis*	28
144	**Ruff**	*Philomachus pugnax*	
145	**Jack Snipe**	*Lymnocryptes minimus*	
146	**Snipe**	*Gallinago gallinago*	
147	Great Snipe	*Gallinago media*	19
148	Long-billed Dowitcher	*Limnodromus scolopaceus*	6
149	**Woodcock**	*Scolopax rusticola*	
150	**Black-tailed Godwit**	*Limosa limosa*	
151	**Bar-tailed Godwit**	*Limosa lapponica*	
152	**Whimbrel**	*Numenius phaeopus*	
153	**Curlew**	*Numenius arquata*	
154	Spotted Redshank	*Tringa erythropus*	
155	**Redshank**	*Tringa totanus*	
156	Marsh Sandpiper	*Tringa stagnatilis*	1
157	**Greenshank**	*Tringa nebularia*	
158	Lesser Yellowlegs	*Tringa flavipes*	4
159	**Green Sandpiper**	*Tringa ochropus*	
160	Wood Sandpiper	*Tringa glareola*	
161	Terek Sandpiper	*Xenus cinereus*	1

Last ac. record	
	Uncommon passage species and rare in winter
1969	Very rare
	Common breeding, passage and wintering species
	Fairly common on passage and in winter
	Fairly common on passage and in winter
2002	Very rare
1998	Very rare
	Uncommon on passage
2011	Rare
2007	Rare
1993	Very rare
	Rare
	Uncommon on passage
	Common on passage and in winter
	Uncommon breeding species, common on passage and in winter
1999	Very rare
2011	Rare
	Fairly common on passage
	Uncommon on passage and in winter
	Common breeding, passage and wintering species
2000	Rare
2004	Very rare
	Fairly common on passage and in winter
	Rare breeding species and fairly common on passage
	Fairly common on passage and in winter
	Rare breeding species and fairly common on passage
	Common breeding species and abundant in winter
	Rare on passage
	Fairly common breeding species, common on passage and in winter
1979	Very rare
	Uncommon on passage, has bred
2007	Very rare
	Uncommon on passage
	Rare on passage
1987	Very rare

No	Species	Scientific Name	occur.
162	**Common Sandpiper**	*Actitis hypoleucos*	
163	Spotted Sandpiper	*Actitis macularius*	3
164	**Turnstone**	*Arenaria interpres*	
165	Wilson's Phalarope	*Phalaropus tricolor*	2
166	**Red-necked Phalarope**	*Phalaropus lobatus*	
167	Grey Phalarope	*Phalaropus fulicarius*	
168	**Pomarine Skua**	*Stercorarius pomarinus*	
169	**Arctic Skua**	*Stercorarius parasiticus*	
170	**Long-tailed Skua**	*Stercorarius longicaudus*	
171	**Great Skua**	*Stercorarius skua*	
172	Mediterranean Gull	*Larus melanocephalus*	26
173	Laughing Gull	*Larus atricilla*	2
174	Franklins Gull	*Larus pipixcan*	1
175	**Little Gull**	*Larus minutus*	
176	Sabine's Gull	*Larus sabini*	
177	**Black-headed Gull**	*Larus ridibundus*	
178	**Ring-billed Gull**	*Larus delawarensis*	
179	**Common Gull**	*Larus canus*	
180	**Lesser Black-backed Gull**	*Larus fuscus*	
181	**Herring Gull**	*Larus argentatus*	
182	Yellow-legged Gull	*L. argentatus michahellis*	7
183	**Iceland Gull**	*Larus glaucoides*	
184	**Glaucous Gull**	*Larus hyperboreus*	
185	**Great Black-backed Gull**	*Larus marinus*	
186	Ross's Gull	*Rhodostethia rosea*	4
187	**Kittiwake**	*Rissa tridactyla*	
188	Ivory Gull	*Pagophila eburnea*	6
189	Gull-billed Tern	*Gelochelidon nilotica*	2
190	Caspian Tern	*Sterna caspia*	1
191	**Sandwich Tern**	*Sterna sandvicensis*	
192	Roseate Tern	*Sterna dougallii*	12
193	**Common Tern**	*Sterna hirundo*	
194	**Arctic Tern**	*Sterna paradisaea*	
195	Forster's Tern	*Sterna forsteri*	1
196	Bridled Tern	*Sterna anaethetus*	1
197	**Little Tern**	*Sterna albifrons*	

Last ac. record	
	Uncommon breeding species and passage visitor
2009	Very rare
	Common on passage and in winter
2002	Very rare
	Rare visitor, has bred
	Rare
	Uncommon on passage
	Common breeding and passage species
	Uncommon on passage
	Common breeding and passage species
2007	Rare
2005	Very rare
2009	Very rare
	Uncommon on passage
	Rare
	Common breeding, passage and wintering species
	Rare
	Common breeding species, abundant on passage and in winter
	Common breeding species, very rare in winter
	Common resident breeding and wintering species
2003	Very rare
	Uncommon in winter
	Uncommon in winter
	Common resident breeding and wintering species
2005	Very rare
	Abundant breeding and passage species
1949	Very rare
1992	Very rare
1998	Very rare
	Fairly common breeding and passage species
2011	Very rare
	Fairly common breeding and passage species
	Abundant breeding and passage species
2001	Very rare
1979	Very rare
	Rare breeding breeding species

No	Species	Scientific Name	occur.
198	Black Tern	*Chlidonias niger*	
199	White-winged Black Tern	*Chlidonias leucopterus*	15
200	**Guillemot**	*Uria aalge*	
201	Brünnich's Guillemot	*Uria lomvia*	7
202	**Razorbill**	*Alca torda*	
203	**Great Auk**	*Pinguinus impennis*	
204	**Black Guillemot**	*Cepphus grylle*	
205	**Little Auk**	*Alle alle*	
206	**Puffin**	*Fratercula arctica*	
207	Pallas's Sandgrouse	*Syrrhaptes paradoxus*	13
208	**Rock Dove**	*Columba livia*	
209	Stock Dove	*Columba oenas*	
210	**Woodpigeon**	*Columba palumbus*	
211	**Collared Dove**	*Streptopelia decaocto*	
212	**Turtle Dove**	*Streptopelia turtur*	
213	Rufous Turtle Dove	*Streptopelia orientalis*	1
214	Great Spotted Cuckoo	*Clamator glandarius*	1
215	**Cuckoo**	*Cuculus canorus*	
216	Yellow-billed Cuckoo	*Coccyzus americanus*	4
217	Barn Owl	*Tyto alba*	19
218	Scops Owl	*Otus scops*	6
219	Snowy Owl	*Bubo scandiacus*	23
220	**Long-eared Owl**	*Asio otus*	
221	**Short-eared Owl**	*Asio flammeus*	
222	Tengmalm's Owl	*Aegolius funereus*	5
223	Nightjar	*Caprimulgus europaeus*	26
224	Nighthawk	*Chordeiles minor*	1
225	Needle-tailed Swift	*Hirundapus caudacutus*	2
226	**Swift**	*Apus apus*	
227	Pallid Swift	*Apus pallidus*	1
228	Alpine Swift	*Apus melba*	3
229	Kingfisher	*Alcedo atthis*	8
230	Bee-eater	*Merops apiaster*	23
231	Roller	*Coracias garrulus*	4
232	Hoopoe	*Upupa epops*	
233	Wryneck	*Jynx torquilla*	
234	Green Woodpecker	*Picus viridis*	1

Last ac. record	
	Rare on passage
2011	Rare
	Abundant breeding species, common on passage and in winter
2001	Very rare
	Common breeding species, uncommon in winter
1813	Extinct
	Common resident breeding species
	Uncommon on passage and in winter
	Abundant breeding species, rare in winter
1888	Rare; irruptive
	Common resident breeding species
	Rare on passage
	Fairly common resident breeding spécies, uncommon on passage
	Fairly common resident breeding species and passage visitor
	Uncommon on passage
2002	Very rare
1959	Very rare
	Rare breeding species, uncommon on passage
2009	Very rare
2009	Rare
1996	Very rare
2009	Rare
	Uncommon on passage and in winter, has bred
	Uncommon resident breeding species and passage visitor
1986	Very rare
2009	Rare
1978	Very rare
1988	Very rare
	Uncommon on passage
1996	Very rare
2010	Very rare
2001	Very rare
2011	Rare
1966	Very rare
	Rare
	Rare
1885	Very rare

No	Species	Scientific Name	occur.
235	**Great Spotted Woodpecker**	*Dendrocopus major*	
236	Red-eyed Vireo	*Vireo olivaceus*	1
237	Calandra Lark	*Melanocorypha calandra*	1
238	Short-toed Lark	*Calandrella brachydactyla*	
239	Woodlark	*Lullula arborea*	9
240	**Skylark**	*Alauda arvensis*	
241	Shore Lark	*Eremophila alpestris*	
242	**Sand Martin**	*Riparia riparia*	
243	Crag Martin	*Ptyonoprogne rupestris*	1
244	**Swallow**	*Hirundo rustica*	
245	Red-rumped Swallow	*Hirundo daurica*	8
246	**House Martin**	*Delichon urbicum*	
247	Richard's Pipit	*Anthus novaeseelandiae*	
248	Tawny Pipit	*Anthus campestris*	3
249	Olive-backed Pipit	*Anthus hodgsoni*	20
250	Tree Pipit	*Anthus trivialis*	
251	Pechora Pipit	*Anthus gustavi*	2
252	**Meadow Pipit**	*Anthus pratensis*	
253	Red-throated Pipit	*Anthus cervinus*	16
254	**Rock Pipit**	*Anthus petrosus*	
255	Water Pipit	*Anthus spinoletta*	2
256	Buff-bellied Pipit	*Anthus rubescens*	2
257	**Yellow Wagtail**	*Motacilla flava*	
258	Citrine Wagtail	*Motacilla citreola*	14
259	**Grey Wagtail**	*Motacilla cinerea*	
260	**Pied Wagtail**	*Motacilla alba yarrellii*	
261	**Waxwing**	*Bombycilla garrulus*	
262	**Dipper**	*Cinclus cinclus*	
263	**Wren**	*Troglodytes troglodytes*	
264	**Dunnock**	*Prunella modularis*	
265	**Robin**	*Erithacus rubecula*	
266	Rufous-tailed Robin	*Luscinia sibilans*	1
267	Thrush Nightingale	*Luscinia luscinia*	7

Last ac. record	
	Uncommon on passage and in winter; irruptive
2009	Very rare
2002	Very rare
	Rare
2010	Very rare
	Common breeding species and on passage, fairly common in winter
	Rare
	Rare breeding species, fairly common on passage
1999	Very rare
	Fairly common breeding species and passage visitor
2010	Very rare
	Uncommon breeding species, fairly common on passage
	Rare
2010	Very rare
2010	Rare
	Uncommon on passage
2005	Very rare
	Common breeding species and on passage, uncommon in winter
1999	Rare
	Fairly common resident breeding species and passage visitor
1996	Very rare
2010	Very rare
	Uncommon passage visitor, has bred
2009	Rare
	Rare breeding species, uncommon on passage and rare in winter
	Fairly common breeding species and passage visitor, rare in winter
	Uncommon on passage and in winter; irruptive
	Rare, has bred
	Common resident breeding species, uncommon on passage
	Uncommon resident breeding species and passage visitor
	Uncommon resident breeding species, fairly common on passage
2010	Very rare
2006	Very rare

No	Species	Scientific Name	occur.
268	Nightingale	*Luscinia megarhynchos*	12
269	**Bluethroat**	*Luscinia svecica*	
270	Siberian Blue Robin	*Luscinia cyane*	1
271	Red-flanked Bluetail	*Tarsiger cyanurus*	2
272	**Black Redstart**	*Phoenicurus ochruros*	
273	**Redstart**	*Phoenicurus phoenicurus*	
274	**Whinchat**	*Saxicola rubetra*	
275	**Stonechat**	*Saxicola torquata*	
276	Isabelline Wheatear	*Oenanthe isabellina*	1
277	**Wheatear**	*Oenanthe oenanthe*	
278	Pied Wheatear	*Oenanthe pleschanka*	7
279	Desert Wheatear	*Oenanthe deserti*	2
280	Rock Thrush	*Monticola saxatilis*	1
281	White's Thrush	*Zoothera dauma*	2
282	Siberian Thrush	*Zoothera sibirica*	2
283	Olive-backed Thrush	*Catharus ustulatus*	1
284	Grey-cheeked Thrush	*Catharus minimus*	2
285	Veery	*Catharus fuscescens*	1
286	**Ring Ouzel**	*Turdus torquatus*	
287	**Blackbird**	*Turdus merula*	
288	Eye-browed Thrush	*Turdus obscurus*	1
289	Black-throated Thrush	*Turdus ruficollis*	4
290	**Fieldfare**	*Turdus pilaris*	
291	**Song Thrush**	*Turdus philomelos*	
292	**Redwing**	*Turdus iliacus*	
293	**Mistle Thrush**	*Turdus viscivorus*	
294	American Robin	*Turdus migratorius*	1
295	Pallas's Grasshopper Warbler	*Locustella certhiola*	1
296	Lanceolated Warbler	*Locustella lanceolata*	4
297	Grasshopper Warbler	*Locustella naevia*	
298	River Warbler	*Locustella fluviatilis*	2
299	Aquatic Warbler	*Acrocephalus paludicola*	1
300	**Sedge Warbler**	*Acrocephalus schoenobaenus*	
301	Paddyfield Warbler	*Acrocephalus agricola*	4
302	Blyth's Reed Warbler	*Acrocephalus dumetorum*	13

Last ac. record	
2011	Rare
	Uncommon on passage
2001	Very rare
2010	Very rare
	Uncommon on passage, has bred
	Uncommon on passage
	Rare breeding species and uncommon on passage
	Uncommon resident breeding species and passage visitor
2005	Very rare
	Fairly common breeding species, common on passage
2010	Very rare
1988	Very rare
1910	Very rare
2003	Very rare
1992	Very rare
1993	Very rare
2001	Very rare
2002	Very rare
	Rare breeding species, fairly common on passage
	Common resident breeding species, on passage and in winter
1984	Very rare
2010	Very rare
	Common on passage and uncommon in winter, has bred
	Uncommon resident breeding species, fairly common on passage
	Abundant on passage and fairly common in winter, has bred
	Uncommon on passage, has bred
1961	Very rare
1992	Very rare
2009	Very rare
	Rare on passage
2008	Very rare
1999	Very rare
	Fairly common breeding species and passage visitor
1997	Very rare
2011	Very rare

No	Species	Scientific Name	occur.
303	Marsh Warbler	*Acrocephalus palustris*	
304	Reed Warbler	*Acrocephalus scirpaceus*	
305	Great Reed Warbler	*Acrocephalus arundinaceus*	3
306	Booted Warbler	*Hippolais caligata*	2
307	Syke's Warbler	*Hippolais rama*	2
308	**Icterine Warbler**	*Hippolais icterina*	
309	Melodious Warbler	*Hippolais polyglotta*	15
310	**Blackcap**	*Sylvia atricapilla*	
311	**Garden Warbler**	*Sylvia borin*	
312	**Lesser Whitethroat**	*Sylvia curruca*	
313	**Whitethroat**	*Sylvia communis*	
314	**Barred Warbler**	*Sylvia nisoria*	
315	Subalpine Warbler	*Sylvia cantillans*	22
316	Sardinian Warbler	*Sylvia melanocephala*	3
317	Greenish Warbler	*Phylloscopus trochiloides*	17
318	Arctic Warbler	*Phylloscopus borealis*	21
319	Pallas's Warbler	*Phylloscopus proregulus*	33
320	**Yellow-browed Warbler**	*Phylloscopus inornatus*	
321	Hume's Warbler	*Phylloscopus humei*	2
322	Radde's Warbler	*Phylloscopus swarzii*	7
323	Dusky Warbler	*Phylloscopus fuscatus*	7
324	Bonelli's Warbler	*Phylloscopus bonelli*	8
325	Wood Warbler	*Phylloscopus sibilatrix*	
326	**Chiffchaff**	*Phylloscopus collybita*	
327	**Willow Warbler**	*Phylloscopus trochilus*	
328	**Goldcrest**	*Regulus regulus*	
329	Firecrest	*Regulus ignicapillus*	22
330	**Spotted Flycatcher**	*Muscicapa striata*	
331	Red-breasted Flycatcher	*Ficedula parva*	
332	Collared Flycatcher	*Ficedula albicollis*	3
333	**Pied Flycatcher**	*Ficedula hypoleuca*	
334	Bearded Tit	*Panurus biarmicus*	1
335	Long-tailed Tit	*Aegithalos caudatus*	
336	Coal Tit	*Parus ater*	
337	Blue Tit	*Parus caeruleus*	
338	Great Tit	*Parus major*	
339	Treecreeper	*Certhia familiaris*	31
340	Golden Oriole	*Oriolus oriolus*	

Last ac. record	
	Rare on passage
	Rare on passage
2004	Very rare
1993	Very rare
2003	Very rare
	Uncommon on passage, has bred
2003	Rare
	Very rare breeding species, common on passage and uncommon in winter
	Very rare breeding species, fairly common on passage
	Very rare breeding species, uncommon on passage
	Very rare breeding species, uncommon on passage
	Uncommon on passage
2011	Rare
1992	Very rare
2008	Rare
2005	Rare
2009	Rare
	Uncommon on passage
2008	Very rare
1997	Very rare
2003	Very rare
2010	Very rare
	Uncommon on passage, has bred
	Fairly common on passage, has bred
	Uncommon breeding species, fairly common on passage
	Uncommon resident breeding species, common on passage
2010	Rare
	Rare breeding species, fairly common on passage
	Rare on passage
1999	Very rare
	Fairly common on passage
1998	Rare
	Rare
	Rare, but first bred in 2010
	Rare
	Rare
2010	Rare
	Rare

No	Species	Scientific Name	occur.
341	Isabelline Shrike	*Lanius isabellinus*	4
342	**Red-backed Shrike**	*Lanius collurio*	
343	Lesser Grey Shrike	*Lanius minor*	4
344	**Great Grey Shrike**	*Lanius excubitor*	
345	Southern Grey Shrike	*Lanius meridionalis*	3
346	Woodchat Shrike	*Lanius senator*	12
347	Jay	*Garrulus glandarius*	1
348	Magpie	*Pica pica*	11
349	Nutcracker	*Nucifraga caryocatactes*	1
350	Chough	*Pyrrhocorax pyrrhocorax*	5
351	**Jackdaw**	*Corvus monedula*	
352	**Rook**	*Corvus frugilegus*	
353	**Carrion Crow**	*Corvus corone*	
354	**Hooded Crow**	*Corvus cornix*	
355	**Raven**	*Corvus corax*	
356	**Starling**	*Sturnus vulgaris*	
357	**Rosy Starling**	*Sturnus roseus*	44
358	**House Sparrow**	*Passer domesticus*	
359	Spanish Sparrow	*Passer hispaniolensis*	1
360	**Tree Sparrow**	*Passer montanus*	
361	**Chaffinch**	*Fringilla coelebs*	
362	**Brambling**	*Fringilla montifringilla*	
363	**Greenfinch**	*Carduelis chloris*	
364	**Goldfinch**	*Carduelis carduelis*	
365	**Siskin**	*Carduelis spinus*	
366	**Linnet**	*Carduelis cannabina*	
367	**Twite**	*Carduelis flavirostris*	
368	**Lesser Redpoll**	*Carduelis cabaret*	
369	**Common Redpoll**	*Carduelis flammea*	
370	Arctic Redpoll	*Carduelis hornemanni*	46
371	Two-barred Crossbill	*Loxia leucoptera*	20
372	**Crossbill**	*Loxia curvirostra*	
373	Parrot Crossbill	*Loxia pytyopsittacus*	3
374	Trumpeter Finch	*Bucanetes githagineus*	1

Last ac. record	
2006	Very rare
	Uncommon on passage
2004	Very rare
	Uncommon on passage
2000	Very rare
2008	Rare
1967	Very rare
2003	Rare
1868	Very rare
2000	Very rare
	Fairly common resident breeding species, uncommon on passage
	Common resident breeding species, uncommon on passage
	Rare resident breeding species, uncommon on passage
	Common resident breeding species, uncommon on passage
	Uncommon resident breeding species and passage visitor
	Common resident breeding species, abundant on passage and in winter
2011	Rare
	Common resident breeding species
1993	Very rare
	Rare on passage, has bred
	Uncommon resident breeding species, fairly common on passage
	Fairly common on passage, uncommon in winter, has bred
	Uncommon resident breeding species, fairly common on passage
	Uncommon on passage and in winter
	Fairly common on passage, has bred
	Fairly common resident breeding species and passage visitor
	Uncommon resident breeding species, common on passage and in winter
	Uncommon on passage, has bred
	Fairly common on passage, has bred
2010	Rare
2011	Very rare
	Uncommon on passage; irruptive
1985	Very rare
1981	Very rare

No	Species	Scientific Name	occur.
375	**Rosefinch**	*Carpodacus erythrinus*	
376	**Bullfinch**	*Pyrrhula pyrrhula*	
377	**Hawfinch**	*Coccothraustes coccothraustes*	
378	Tennessee Warbler	*Vermivora peregrina*	1
379	Yellow Warbler	*Dendroica petechia*	1
380	Yellow-rumped Warbler	*Dendroica coronata*	2
381	White-throated Sparrow	*Zonotrichia albicollis*	1
382	Dark-eyed Junco	*Junco hyemalis*	1
383	**Lapland Bunting**	*Calcarius lapponicus*	
384	**Snow Bunting**	*Plectrophenax nivalis*	
385	Pine Bunting	*Emberiza leucocephalos*	11
386	**Yellowhammer**	*Emberiza citrinella*	
387	Cirl Bunting	*Emberiza cirlus*	3
388	Ortolan Bunting	*Emberiza hortulana*	
389	Cretzschmar's Bunting	*Emberiza caesia*	2
390	Yellow-browed Bunting	*Emberiza chrysophrys*	2
391	Rustic Bunting	*Emberiza rustica*	30
392	Little Bunting	*Emberiza pusilla*	
393	Yellow-breasted Bunting	*Emberiza aureola*	9
394	**Reed Bunting**	*Emberiza schoeniclus*	
395	Black-headed Bunting	*Emberiza melanocephala*	11
396	**Corn Bunting**	*Emberiza calandra*	
	Category D		
	Red-breasted Goose	*Branta ruficollis*	
	Falcated Duck	*Anas falcata*	
	Booted Eagle	*Hieraaetus pennatus*	
	Saker Falcon	*Falco cherrug*	
	Blue Rock Thrush	*Monticola solitarius*	
	Red-headed Bunting	*Emberiza bruniceps*	
	Category E		
	Chilean Flamingo	*Phoenicopterus chilensis*	
	Black Swan	*Cygnus atratus*	
	Bar-headed Goose	*Anser indicus*	
	Demoiselle Crane	*Anthropoides virgo*	
	Eagle Owl	*Bubo bubo*	
	Pallas's Rosefinch	*Carpodacus roseus*	
	Lazuli Bunting	*Passerina amoena*	

Last ac. record	
	Uncommon on passage
	Uncommon on passage and in winter
	Rare on passage
1982	Very rare
1992	Very rare
2003	Very rare
1996	Very rare
2007	Very rare
	Uncommon on passage
	Common on passage and in winter
1995	Rare
	Uncommon on passage, rare in winter, has bred
2003	Very rare
	Rare on passage
2008	Very rare
1998	Very rare
2010	Rare
	Rare on passage
2003	Very rare
	Fairly common resident breeding species and passage visitor
2003	Rare
	Very rare on passage, has bred
2004	
2000	
2000	
1966	
1989	
1974	
2002	
1863	
1830	
1988	
1964	

Bibliography

Baikie, W.B. and Heddle, R. (1848) *Historia Naturalis Orcadensis. Zoology, Part 1*. Paterson, Edinburgh.

Balfour, E. (1967) *Orkney Birds Status and Guide*. Stromness, Orkney.

Berry, R.J. (1985) *The Natural History of Orkney.* Collins New Naturalist, London.

Berry, R.J. (2000) *Orkney Nature,* T & A.D.Poyser

Cramp, S & Simmons, K.E.L.(eds) (1977) *The Birds of the Western Palearctic Vols 1- 10*. Oxford University Press.

Booth, C.J., Cuthbert, Mildred and Reynolds, P. (1984) *The Birds of Orkney*. Orkney Press, Stromness.

Booth, C. and Booth, J. (1998) *Status and Checklist of The Vertebrate Fauna of Orkney*. C&J Booth, Kirkwall.

Booth, Chris and Booth, Jean. (2005) *Sillocks, Skarfies and Selkies, The Vertebrate Fauna of Orkney.* The Orcadian, Kirkwall.

Cocker, Mark and Mabey, Richard (2005) *Birds Britannica.* Chatto and Windus, London.

Flaws, Margaret and Woodford, Bridget (1997) *Teeos and Tea-flooers*. Pinnsvin, Wyre, Orkney.

Gibbons, D.W., Reid, J.B. & Chapman, R.A. (1993) *The New Atlas of Breeding Birds in Britain and Ireland: 1988-1991*. T & A.D.Poyser, London.

Greenoak Francesca (1979) *All the Birds of the Air*. Penguin, England.

Groundwater William (1974) *Birds and Mammals of Orkney*. Kirkwall Press, Kirkwall.

Lack, Peter (1986) *The Atlas of Wintering Birds in Britain and Ireland*. T&A.D.Poyser, Calton.

Lamb Gregor (1988) *Orkney Wordbook*. Kirkwall Press, Kirkwall.

Meek Eric (1985) *Islands of Birds, a Guide to Orkney Birds*. RSPB.

Orkney Bird Reports, 1980 to 2006. Orkney Bird Report Committee.

Sharrock, J.T.R. (1976) *The Atlas of Breeding Birds in Britain and Ireland*. T&A.D.Poyser, Berkhamsted.

Stanek, V.J, *Birds of Field and Forest*. Spring Books, London.

Tait Charles, *The Orkney Guide Book*. Charles Tait, Photographic, Orkney.

Tay and Orkney Ringing Groups (1984) *The Shore birds of the Orkney Islands.* Tay Ringing Group, Perth.

Index

Notes:

Notes:

Notes:

Notes: